# TCP/IP

## *NETWORK+ PROTOCOLS AND CAMPUS LAN SWITCHING FUNDAMENTALS*

## 4 BOOKS IN 1

### BOOK 1
*TCP/IP ESSENTIALS: A BEGINNER'S GUIDE*

### BOOK 2
*NETWORK+ PROTOCOLS: INTERMEDIATE INSIGHTS*

### BOOK 3
*ADVANCED TCP/IP AND CAMPUS LAN SWITCHING*

### BOOK 4
*EXPERT TCP/IP OPTIMIZATION AND TROUBLESHOOTING*

## *ROB BOTWRIGHT*

*Published by Rob Botwright*
*Library of Congress Cataloging-in-Publication Data*
*ISBN 978-1-83938-665-7*
*Cover design by Rizzo*

*Disclaimer*

*The contents of this book are based on extensive research and the best available historical sources. However, the author and publisher make no claims, promises, or guarantees about the accuracy, completeness, or adequacy of the information contained herein. The information in this book is provided on an "as is" basis, and the author and publisher disclaim any and all liability for any errors, omissions, or inaccuracies in the information or for any actions taken in reliance on such information. The opinions and views expressed in this book are those of the author and do not necessarily reflect the official policy or position of any organization or individual mentioned in this book. Any reference to specific people, places, or events is intended only to provide historical context and is not intended to defame or malign any group, individual, or entity. The information in this book is intended for educational and entertainment purposes only. It is not intended to be a substitute for professional advice or judgment. Readers are encouraged to conduct their own research and to seek professional advice where appropriate. Every effort has been made to obtain necessary permissions and acknowledgments for all images and other copyrighted material used in this book. Any errors or omissions in this regard are unintentional, and the author and publisher will correct them in future editions.*

## Introduction

In the ever-connected world of today, the field of networking is the backbone of our digital existence. From the smallest devices to the grandest data centers, networks facilitate the exchange of information that drives our modern lives. At the core of this interconnected universe is the TCP/IP protocol suite, a fundamental pillar that ensures the seamless flow of data across the global network landscape.

The book bundle you are about to embark on, "TCP/IP Network+ Protocols and Campus LAN Switching Fundamentals," is a comprehensive journey through the intricacies of TCP/IP networking, designed to empower learners and professionals alike. Comprising four distinct volumes, each book is meticulously crafted to cater to various levels of expertise, from beginner to expert.

In "TCP/IP Essentials: A Beginner's Guide," Book 1, we start at the very beginning, where networking novices take their first steps into the captivating realm of TCP/IP. This beginner's guide serves as the foundation upon which your networking knowledge will be built. It demystifies the TCP/IP protocol suite, breaking down complex concepts into digestible pieces, and introduces you to IP addressing and the core principles that underpin modern networks.

Moving forward, "Network+ Protocols: Intermediate Insights," Book 2, bridges the gap between basic understanding and intermediate expertise. As you progress through this volume, you'll delve deeper into networking protocols, subnetting techniques, and routing concepts. This intermediate insight will equip you with valuable knowledge and tools to design, configure, and manage networks effectively.

Book 3, "Advanced TCP/IP and Campus LAN Switching," is where we venture into advanced territory. Here, we explore intricate topics such as routing protocols, VLAN design, and high availability strategies. This volume is tailored to those who seek to build and secure complex networks that span across campuses and enterprises.

The final frontier awaits in "Expert TCP/IP Optimization and Troubleshooting," Book 4. For seasoned professionals looking to sharpen their skills, this book offers in-depth insights into network optimization, performance tuning, and troubleshooting methodologies. With real-world scenarios and challenges, you'll elevate your TCP/IP proficiency to an expert level.

Each book within this bundle is crafted with the utmost care, ensuring that learners and professionals have access to a wealth of knowledge and practical guidance. The journey through these volumes will take you from a novice exploring the basics to a proficient expert capable of optimizing and troubleshooting complex network environments.

Whether you are new to the world of networking or a seasoned professional seeking to deepen your expertise, the "TCP/IP Network+ Protocols and Campus LAN Switching Fundamentals" bundle is your compass to navigate the ever-evolving landscape of networking technology. Embrace the knowledge within these pages, and embark on a journey that will enable you to thrive in the dynamic world of TCP/IP networking.

*BOOK 1*
*TCP/IP ESSENTIALS*
*A BEGINNER'S GUIDE*

**ROB BOTWRIGHT**

## Chapter 1: Introduction to Networking

Networking fundamentals are the building blocks of modern communication, enabling devices to connect and exchange data seamlessly across vast distances. At its core, networking is about the interconnection of devices, be it computers, smartphones, servers, or other smart appliances, allowing them to share information and resources. To understand networking fully, it's essential to delve into its fundamental concepts, protocols, and technologies.

One of the most critical aspects of networking is the concept of data transmission. Data is exchanged between devices in the form of packets, which are discrete units of information. These packets travel over a network infrastructure, such as cables or wireless connections, guided by a set of rules and conventions known as network protocols. The Transmission Control Protocol (TCP) and Internet Protocol (IP) are two of the most fundamental and widely used protocols in networking.

IP addresses play a vital role in networking, serving as unique identifiers for devices on a network. An IP address is akin to a street address for a house; it allows data to be routed to the correct destination. IPv4, the fourth version of the Internet Protocol, uses a 32-bit address format, resulting in approximately 4.3 billion unique addresses. IPv6, on the other hand, employs a 128-bit address format, providing an almost inexhaustible number of unique addresses to accommodate the growing number of devices connected to the internet.

Subnetting is a technique used to divide an IP network into smaller, more manageable subnetworks or subnets. This practice helps in optimizing IP address allocation and facilitates efficient network management. To create subnets, network administrators utilize subnet masks and perform bitwise operations to determine which portion of the IP address represents the network and which part identifies individual devices.

Understanding the hierarchy of IP addresses is crucial. Classful IP addressing, based on the first few bits of an IP address, originally divided addresses into five classes: A, B, C, D, and E. Classes A, B, and C were primarily used for host addressing, while Class D was reserved for multicast groups, and Class E was reserved for experimental purposes. However, with the advent of Classless Inter-Domain Routing (CIDR), these traditional classes have become less relevant. CIDR allows for more flexible allocation of IP address ranges.

To configure network devices and ensure proper communication, network administrators often employ the command-line interface (CLI). CLI commands enable the configuration of routers, switches, firewalls, and other network equipment. For instance, configuring an IP address on a network interface of a router might involve using commands like "interface GigabitEthernet0/0" and "ip address 192.168.1.1 255.255.255.0."

Routers play a critical role in directing data traffic between different networks. They examine the destination IP address of incoming packets and determine the most suitable path for forwarding them to their intended destinations. Routing tables within routers store information about known networks and their associated next-hop routers, helping in the decision-making process.

Switches, on the other hand, operate at the data link layer and are responsible for forwarding Ethernet frames within a local area network (LAN). Unlike routers, switches do not make decisions based on IP addresses; instead, they use MAC (Media Access Control) addresses to identify and forward frames to their intended recipients within the same LAN.

To ensure secure and efficient data transmission, network protocols employ various mechanisms for error detection and correction. One such mechanism is the use of checksums or cyclic redundancy checks (CRCs) to detect errors in transmitted data. If errors are detected, the data is retransmitted to ensure its integrity.

Virtual Private Networks (VPNs) are essential for secure communication over public networks, such as the internet. VPNs create encrypted tunnels that protect data as it travels from one network to another. They are widely used by remote workers to connect securely to their organization's network and by individuals to safeguard their online privacy.

Firewalls are another crucial component of network security. They act as barriers between an internal network and external threats, such as unauthorized access or malicious traffic. Firewalls examine incoming and outgoing data packets and apply predefined rules to determine whether to allow or block them. Configuring firewall rules is a critical task to ensure that only legitimate traffic passes through.

Intrusion Detection Systems (IDS) and Intrusion Prevention Systems (IPS) are tools used to monitor network traffic for suspicious or malicious activities. IDSs analyze network traffic patterns and raise alerts when potentially harmful activities are detected. IPSs, on the other hand, can not only detect but also take proactive measures to block or mitigate security threats in real-time.

Wireless networking has become ubiquitous, enabling users to connect to the internet and local networks without physical cables. Common wireless standards, such as Wi-Fi (802.11), provide high-speed connectivity within a limited range. Securing wireless networks is essential to prevent unauthorized access, and techniques like WPA3 encryption and MAC filtering are commonly employed.

Quality of Service (QoS) is a network management technique used to prioritize and allocate network resources based on the importance of data traffic. QoS ensures that critical applications, such as VoIP calls or video conferencing, receive the necessary bandwidth and low latency while less critical traffic may experience delays.

In modern networking, cloud integration and hybrid networks are prevalent. Organizations often use cloud services for scalability, cost-efficiency, and flexibility. Hybrid networks seamlessly combine on-premises infrastructure with cloud resources, allowing for a hybrid IT environment. Configuration and management of hybrid networks involve coordinating on-premises equipment with cloud resources through cloud service providers' interfaces.

As networks continue to evolve, network automation and DevOps practices gain significance. Automation tools and scripts help streamline network management tasks, reducing manual errors and improving efficiency. Infrastructure as Code (IaC) is a methodology used to define and provision network resources through code, enabling rapid deployment and scaling of network infrastructure.

Real-world scenarios and case studies are invaluable in understanding complex network troubleshooting. Network professionals often encounter challenging issues that require a systematic approach to identify and resolve. Case studies provide practical insights into diagnosing and mitigating network problems, enhancing the skills of network administrators and engineers.

In summary, networking fundamentals encompass a wide array of concepts, technologies, and protocols that underpin the functioning of modern communication systems. From the basics of data transmission and IP addressing to advanced topics like security, QoS, and cloud integration, a solid understanding of these fundamentals is essential for network professionals to design, deploy, and maintain reliable and efficient networks in today's interconnected world.

The historical development of networking is a fascinating journey that traces the evolution of human communication and connectivity. It spans centuries, with each era introducing innovative technologies and concepts that have paved the way for our modern interconnected world.

In ancient times, human communication was limited to face-to-face interactions, written messages, and the use of smoke signals or drumbeats to convey information over long distances. These methods were effective for their time but had severe limitations in terms of speed and reach.

One of the earliest breakthroughs in long-distance communication was the invention of the telegraph in the early 19th century. Samuel Morse's Morse code enabled the transmission of messages over electrical wires, revolutionizing communication by allowing near-instantaneous transmission of information across great distances.

The telegraph's success laid the foundation for the development of the first global communication network, the undersea telegraph cable system. This system used insulated cables laid on the ocean floor to connect continents, reducing the time it took to send messages from weeks or months to mere minutes. One of the most famous achievements of this era was the laying of the first transatlantic telegraph cable in 1858, connecting Europe and North America.

In parallel with the telegraph, another significant development was taking shape in the form of the telephone.

Alexander Graham Bell's invention of the telephone in 1876 marked a milestone in the history of voice communication. The telephone network quickly expanded, connecting homes and businesses, and eventually leading to the creation of the first telephone exchanges.

The advent of the 20th century brought about the age of radio communication. Radio waves enabled wireless communication, making it possible to transmit voice and later data over the airwaves. Marconi's wireless telegraphy system was among the earliest implementations of radio communication, enabling ships to communicate with each other and with shore stations.

During World War II, significant advancements were made in the field of electronics and communication. The development of radar and encryption technologies played pivotal roles in military operations, setting the stage for later developments in civilian communications.

After the war, the world witnessed the birth of the computer age. Early computers were massive, room-sized machines with limited processing power. However, they marked the beginning of a new era in data processing and communication. One of the key figures in this era was Claude Shannon, who laid the groundwork for digital circuit design and information theory.

The 1960s saw the emergence of computer networks. The Advanced Research Projects Agency Network (ARPANET), funded by the U.S. Department of Defense, was one of the earliest examples of a computer network. ARPANET was designed to facilitate communication and resource sharing among researchers, serving as a precursor to the modern internet.

In the 1970s, the development of the Transmission Control Protocol (TCP) and Internet Protocol (IP) by Vinton Cerf and Robert Kahn laid the foundation for the modern internet.

These protocols established the rules for packet-switching and data transmission across interconnected networks. The adoption of TCP/IP as the standard protocol suite for the ARPANET marked the birth of the internet as we know it today.

The 1980s and 1990s witnessed the rapid expansion of the internet, driven by advancements in networking technologies and the development of the World Wide Web (WWW) by Tim Berners-Lee. The WWW made it possible for people to access information and services over the internet through web browsers, opening up new possibilities for communication, commerce, and collaboration.

The commercialization of the internet in the 1990s led to the proliferation of internet service providers (ISPs) and the establishment of the World Wide Web Consortium (W3C), which standardized web technologies. E-commerce, email, and instant messaging became integral parts of daily life, reshaping the way people communicated and conducted business.

The 21st century has been marked by the explosion of digital technologies and the continuous evolution of networking. High-speed broadband internet, wireless networks, and mobile devices have made it possible for people to be connected virtually anytime and anywhere. The Internet of Things (IoT) has extended the reach of networking to everyday objects, creating a networked ecosystem of smart devices.

Cloud computing has transformed the way data and applications are hosted and accessed, offering scalability and flexibility to businesses and individuals alike. Virtual private networks (VPNs) and secure communication protocols have become essential for protecting data privacy and security in an increasingly connected world.

The historical development of networking has been a journey of human innovation and ingenuity. From the humble beginnings of smoke signals and telegraphs to the vast, interconnected web of today, networking has reshaped the way we communicate, collaborate, and share information. It continues to evolve, with emerging technologies such as 5G, artificial intelligence, and blockchain promising to redefine the possibilities of networking in the future.

As we reflect on the historical milestones and technological advancements that have brought us to this point, it is clear that networking has become an integral part of our daily lives, shaping the way we work, play, and connect with the world around us. The journey of networking is far from over, and the next chapter promises even greater innovations and opportunities for the future.

## Chapter 2: Understanding the TCP/IP Protocol Suite

In the world of computer networking, two fundamental models are used to describe and understand how data is transmitted and processed across networks: the OSI (Open Systems Interconnection) model and the TCP/IP (Transmission Control Protocol/Internet Protocol) model.

The OSI model and the TCP/IP model are both conceptual frameworks that help network engineers and professionals understand and standardize network communication. They provide a structured way to discuss and analyze the different layers of network functionality and how they interact.

The OSI model, developed by the International Organization for Standardization (ISO), was introduced in the late 1970s. It consists of seven layers, each with a specific function and responsibility in the process of transmitting data from one device to another.

The TCP/IP model, on the other hand, is a more simplified model that was developed to describe the functioning of the internet and the protocols used in the early stages of its development. It is often referred to as the Internet Protocol Suite and consists of four layers, which correlate with some of the layers in the OSI model.

Let's explore the OSI model first. The OSI model is a comprehensive framework that divides the networking process into seven layers, starting from the physical layer at the bottom and moving up to the application layer at the top.

The Physical layer, which is Layer 1, deals with the actual physical medium used to transmit data, such as cables, connectors, and electrical or optical signals.

Above the Physical layer is the Data Link layer (Layer 2), responsible for creating a reliable link between two directly connected nodes, often involving data framing and error detection.

The Network layer (Layer 3) focuses on routing and forwarding data packets across different networks. This layer is where IP addresses come into play, and routers operate.

Moving up, the Transport layer (Layer 4) ensures end-to-end communication between devices. It's responsible for segmentation, flow control, and error correction.

The Session layer (Layer 5) manages the establishment, maintenance, and termination of communication sessions between applications on different devices.

The Presentation layer (Layer 6) deals with data translation and encryption, ensuring that data is presented in a format that both sender and receiver can understand.

Finally, the Application layer (Layer 7) is where end-user applications interact with the network. This layer includes protocols for services like email, file transfer, and remote access.

Now, let's turn our attention to the TCP/IP model, which is often compared to the OSI model due to its significance in the development of the internet.

The TCP/IP model consists of four layers, which align with some of the layers in the OSI model, but with differences in terminology and function.

At the bottom of the TCP/IP model is the Network Interface layer, similar to the Data Link and Physical layers in the OSI model. This layer handles the physical and data link aspects of network communication, such as Ethernet or Wi-Fi.

Above the Network Interface layer is the Internet layer, which corresponds to the Network layer in the OSI model. The Internet layer is primarily responsible for routing packets based on IP addresses and handling logical addressing.

Next is the Transport layer, mirroring the Transport layer in the OSI model. It ensures reliable end-to-end communication, just like in the OSI model, and includes protocols like TCP and UDP.

Finally, the Application layer in the TCP/IP model combines elements from the OSI model's Session, Presentation, and Application layers. It encompasses all application-level protocols and interactions, including web browsing, email, and file transfer.

It's important to note that the TCP/IP model is often seen as a more practical and directly applicable model for understanding internet-based networking because it was designed with the specific needs of the internet in mind. In contrast, the OSI model is more theoretical and serves as a general framework for understanding network protocols and concepts.

While the OSI model provides a more detailed breakdown of networking functions into seven distinct layers, the TCP/IP model is more streamlined, making it easier to understand how the internet works at a high level.

To illustrate the relationship between the two models, you can think of the four layers in the TCP/IP model as a condensed version of the seven layers in the OSI model, with some layers having a direct one-to-one correspondence, such as the Network and Transport layers.

In practice, when troubleshooting network issues or configuring network equipment, network professionals often refer to both models to better understand the various layers and protocols involved in the communication process.

For example, when configuring a router using the command-line interface (CLI), a network engineer might enter commands like "ip route" to configure routing in the Network layer, or "access-list" to define access control in the Transport layer, depending on the specific task.

Understanding both models is essential for network professionals because they provide valuable insights into how networks operate and how different protocols and technologies fit together to enable communication across the internet and other networks.

In summary, the OSI model and the TCP/IP model are two complementary frameworks that help us understand the complex world of computer networking. While the OSI model offers a more detailed and theoretical view, the TCP/IP model provides a practical and simplified perspective that aligns closely with the internet's architecture. Together, these models provide a comprehensive foundation for comprehending the intricacies of network communication and protocol interaction.

In the realm of computer networking, the TCP/IP protocol suite plays a central and indispensable role, providing the essential framework for data transmission and communication over networks. At its core, the TCP/IP suite is organized into layers, each with a specific function and responsibility, forming a structured hierarchy that governs how data is prepared, transmitted, and received.

The TCP/IP protocol suite consists of four primary layers, each serving a unique purpose in the process of data exchange. These layers, from the bottom up, are the Network Interface Layer, the Internet Layer, the Transport Layer, and the Application Layer.

Starting at the lowest layer, the Network Interface Layer deals with the physical and data link aspects of networking. It encompasses the physical medium over which data is transmitted, whether it's copper or fiber-optic cables, wireless radio waves, or other transmission media. Additionally, this layer manages the addressing and framing of data for local network communication.

The Network Interface Layer involves devices such as network interface cards (NICs), switches, and routers. NICs are responsible for converting digital data from the computer into signals suitable for transmission over the network medium and vice versa. Switches operate at this layer, making decisions based on MAC (Media Access Control) addresses to forward data frames within a local network, while routers extend this functionality to route data between different networks.

Moving up one layer, we encounter the Internet Layer, often referred to as the heart of the TCP/IP suite. The primary responsibility of this layer is the routing of data packets across networks. It does so by using logical addressing, represented by IP (Internet Protocol) addresses. IP addresses serve as unique identifiers for devices on a network, enabling routers to determine the appropriate path for data packets.

The Internet Layer deals with devices like routers, which are essential for directing data traffic between different networks. Routing tables within routers store information about known networks and the next-hop routers that should be used for forwarding data. IP addresses also help routers make these routing decisions efficiently.

Above the Internet Layer is the Transport Layer, which ensures end-to-end communication between devices and applications. It accomplishes this by providing mechanisms for segmentation, flow control, error detection, and error correction. Two of the most well-known protocols at this layer are the Transmission Control Protocol (TCP) and the User Datagram Protocol (UDP).

TCP is a connection-oriented protocol that guarantees reliable and ordered data delivery. It establishes a connection between the sender and receiver, maintains flow control to prevent congestion, and retransmits lost or corrupted data to ensure complete and accurate delivery. In contrast, UDP is connectionless and offers minimal services. While it is faster and places less overhead on the network, it does not guarantee delivery or ensure the order of transmitted data.

The Transport Layer is crucial for applications that require a reliable data exchange, such as web browsing, email, and file transfers. It also handles the multiplexing of multiple application-layer protocols over a single network connection.

Finally, at the top layer, we find the Application Layer. This layer is where end-user applications and services interact with the network. It encompasses a wide range of application-specific protocols and services, including HTTP for web browsing, SMTP for email, FTP for file transfers, and DNS for domain name resolution.

The Application Layer protocols define how data is formatted, presented, and processed for specific applications. For instance, the HTTP protocol specifies how web browsers request and receive web pages, while the FTP protocol outlines the steps for transferring files between a client and server.

The Application Layer is where network administrators and developers interact most directly with the TCP/IP suite, configuring and managing the protocols and services that facilitate communication between users and applications.

To illustrate how these layers work together, let's consider a typical scenario of visiting a website. At the Application Layer, a web browser initiates a request to retrieve a web page. This request is formatted according to the HTTP protocol.

As the request descends through the layers, it is segmented into packets at the Transport Layer, using either TCP or UDP as the transport protocol. TCP might be chosen to ensure the reliable delivery of the web page's content.

At the Internet Layer, the packets are routed based on their destination IP address, traveling across different networks if necessary. Routers at this layer make forwarding decisions to guide the packets to the correct destination.

Finally, at the Network Interface Layer, the packets are prepared for transmission over the physical medium, such as an Ethernet cable or a wireless connection, and are sent to the destination's MAC address.

Upon reaching the destination, the process is reversed, with the packets traveling back up through the layers. At the Application Layer, the web browser receives the web page's content and renders it for the user.

This structured layering of the TCP/IP protocol suite allows for modularity and flexibility in network design and operation. Each layer focuses on specific tasks, and changes or improvements made to one layer do not necessarily affect the others. This separation of concerns contributes to the suite's robustness and adaptability in diverse networking environments.

In practical terms, network professionals often interact with the TCP/IP suite through command-line interfaces (CLIs) or graphical user interfaces (GUIs) to configure devices, troubleshoot connectivity issues, and manage network services. For instance, configuring an IP address on a network interface may involve CLI commands like "ip address" or "ifconfig," depending on the operating system and networking equipment being used.

## Chapter 3: IP Addressing and Subnetting

In the realm of computer networking, IPv4, short for Internet Protocol version 4, is a cornerstone of the internet and local area networks (LANs). IPv4 addresses are numerical labels assigned to devices connected to a network, allowing them to communicate and exchange data. Understanding IPv4 address types is essential for network administrators and professionals, as it plays a crucial role in IP addressing and routing.

IPv4 addresses are divided into various types, each serving a specific purpose in network communication. These address types include unicast, multicast, broadcast, and special-purpose addresses.

Unicast addresses are perhaps the most familiar and widely used IPv4 address type. A unicast address identifies a single network interface, allowing one-to-one communication between the sender and receiver. When you access a website, send an email, or ping a network device, you are typically using unicast addressing. Unicast addresses are essential for point-to-point communication and are the foundation of most internet and LAN traffic.

Multicast addresses, on the other hand, enable one-to-many or many-to-many communication. With multicast addressing, a single packet can be sent to multiple recipients simultaneously, making it an efficient way to distribute data to a specific group of devices. Multicast is commonly used for streaming video and audio, as well as for various network protocols that require group communication. To deploy multicast, network administrators often configure devices to join multicast groups, and routers are responsible for forwarding multicast traffic to the appropriate group members.

Broadcast addresses were once a fundamental part of IPv4 networking, allowing one-to-all communication within a local network segment. When a device sent a broadcast packet, every device on the same network segment would receive and process it. However, due to scalability and security concerns, broadcast addressing has become less common in modern networks. Instead, network administrators often rely on more efficient unicast and multicast addressing to achieve the desired communication.

Special-purpose addresses are a category of IPv4 addresses reserved for specific network functions and scenarios. These addresses are not assigned to individual devices and cannot be used for general communication. Instead, they serve particular purposes within the networking infrastructure.

One well-known special-purpose address is the loopback address, represented as 127.0.0.1 in IPv4. The loopback address is used to test network connectivity on a local device without actually transmitting data over the network. When a device sends data to the loopback address, it is routed back to itself, allowing applications to verify that network services are functioning correctly.

Another special-purpose address is the network address, often represented as the lowest address in a network's address range. For example, in a network with the address range 192.168.1.0/24, the network address would be 192.168.1.0. The network address is not assigned to any specific device and is used as a reference point to identify the network itself.

The broadcast address, while less commonly used today, is also considered a special-purpose address. It typically represents the highest address in a network's address range. For instance, in the same network with the address range

192.168.1.0/24, the broadcast address would be 192.168.1.255. Broadcast addresses are used for sending data packets to all devices within a network segment simultaneously.

Additionally, reserved address ranges exist within IPv4 to cater to specific needs and avoid conflicts. For instance, the range 10.0.0.0 to 10.255.255.255 is reserved for private networks and is commonly used in conjunction with Network Address Translation (NAT) to allow multiple devices on a private network to share a single public IP address.

Similarly, the range 169.254.0.0 to 169.254.255.255 is reserved for Automatic Private IP Addressing (APIPA). When a device is unable to obtain a valid IP address from a DHCP server, it may assign itself an IP address from this reserved range, allowing it to communicate with other devices on the same network segment. Understanding IPv4 address types is vital for network administrators and professionals when designing, configuring, and troubleshooting network infrastructure. Proper addressing ensures efficient and reliable communication across networks, while special-purpose addresses and reserved ranges serve specific networking functions and requirements. Network administrators often interact with these address types through command-line interfaces (CLIs) when configuring devices, setting up routing tables, or troubleshooting network issues. For example, configuring a multicast address for a specific application might involve CLI commands such as "ip multicast-group" or "igmp join-group," depending on the networking equipment and protocols in use. Overall, a comprehensive knowledge of IPv4 address types is essential for building and maintaining robust and efficient networks in today's interconnected world. Subnetting is a fundamental concept in computer networking that allows network administrators to divide a large IP network into smaller, more manageable subnetworks. This technique is essential for efficient IP address allocation and optimizing network performance. Subnetting helps organizations make the most of their IP address space while facilitating efficient routing and minimizing broadcast traffic.

The primary goal of subnetting is to break down a large IP network, often referred to as a classful network, into smaller, more granular subnetworks. This process involves partitioning the available IP addresses into distinct groups, known as subnets, each serving a specific purpose within the organization's network architecture.

One of the most common reasons for subnetting is IP address conservation. In the early days of the internet, IP addresses were allocated based on a classful addressing scheme, which led to inefficient use of address space. Subnetting allows organizations to reclaim unused IP addresses within a classful network and allocate them to subnets as needed.

Another critical benefit of subnetting is network segmentation. By dividing a large network into smaller subnets, organizations can create logical boundaries that improve network management and security. Each subnet can have its own set of policies, access controls, and routing rules, making it easier to control and monitor traffic within and between subnets.

To perform subnetting effectively, network administrators need to understand the concept of subnet masks. A subnet mask is a 32-bit value that consists of ones (1s) and zeros (0s) and is used to distinguish the network portion of an IP address from the host portion. The subnet mask is applied to an IP address using a bitwise AND operation, resulting in the network address.

For example, consider an IP address of 192.168.1.1 with a subnet mask of 255.255.255.0. When the subnet mask is applied, the network address becomes 192.168.1.0, and the host portion remains as 1. This means that all IP addresses in the range 192.168.1.1 to 192.168.1.254 belong to the same subnet.

Subnet masks can vary in length, and the length of the subnet mask determines the size of the subnet and the number of available IP addresses within it. Longer subnet masks create smaller subnets with fewer host addresses, while shorter subnet masks result in larger subnets with more host addresses.

To calculate the number of subnets and hosts within each subnet, network administrators often use CIDR (Classless Inter-Domain Routing) notation. CIDR notation expresses the subnet mask as a prefix length, represented by a forward slash followed by the number of bits set to 1 in the subnet mask. For example, a subnet mask of 255.255.255.0 is equivalent to a CIDR notation of /24.

CIDR notation provides a more flexible way to define subnets, allowing network administrators to create subnets of varying sizes to meet their specific requirements. It also simplifies routing by aggregating multiple subnets into a single routing entry, reducing the size of routing tables.

When subnetting a network, one common technique is to use subnet masks that result in subnets with a power of two $(2^n)$ available host addresses. This approach simplifies addressing and subnet management, as each subnet will have a consistent number of host addresses.

For example, with a subnet mask of 255.255.255.128 (/25 in CIDR notation), each subnet can accommodate 128 host addresses, ranging from 0 to 127 and 128 to 255. This consistent pattern of subnet sizes makes it easier to allocate IP addresses and manage subnets.

To calculate the number of subnets and hosts within each subnet, you can use the following formulas:

Number of Subnets = 2^(subnet prefix length)
Number of Hosts per Subnet = 2^(32 - subnet prefix length) - 2

The "-2" in the second formula accounts for the network address (all host bits set to 0) and the broadcast address (all host bits set to 1), which cannot be assigned to individual hosts.

For example, with a /25 subnet mask, you have 2^7 = 128 subnets and 2^(32 - 25) - 2 = 126 usable host addresses per subnet.

In practical terms, subnetting is often employed when deploying or managing IP networks, whether in enterprise environments or service provider networks. Network administrators configure routers, switches, and other networking devices to route traffic between subnets, ensuring that communication flows smoothly within and between subnets.

Command-line interfaces (CLIs) are frequently used to configure and manage subnets on network devices. For instance, on a Cisco router, you might use commands like "ip address" and "subnet mask" to assign IP addresses and subnet masks to router interfaces. Additionally, routing protocols like OSPF and BGP are configured to exchange routing information and make subnetted networks reachable.

Subnetting is a versatile technique that empowers network administrators to design and scale their networks efficiently. Whether it's optimizing IP address utilization, improving network security through segmentation, or simplifying routing, subnetting plays a vital role in modern networking, ensuring that networks remain adaptable and responsive to evolving demands.

## Chapter 4: Basic Network Configuration

Configuring routers and switches is a fundamental task for network administrators, as these devices play a pivotal role in determining how data flows within a network. Routers and switches are key components that enable data to traverse networks efficiently, and their proper configuration is crucial for network reliability and performance.

Routers, often considered the traffic directors of a network, are responsible for determining the optimal path for data to travel from one network segment to another. They operate at the network layer (Layer 3) of the OSI model, making routing decisions based on destination IP addresses.

To configure a router, network administrators use command-line interfaces (CLIs) or graphical user interfaces (GUIs) provided by the router's operating system. One common CLI is Cisco's IOS (Internetwork Operating System), used on many Cisco routers. In the CLI, commands are entered to set parameters such as IP addresses on router interfaces, configure routing protocols, create access control lists (ACLs) for security, and establish virtual private networks (VPNs).

For example, to configure an IP address on a router interface, the "ip address" command is used, specifying the IP address and subnet mask. To enable routing between subnets, administrators configure routing protocols such as OSPF or EIGRP. The "router ospf" command is used to enter OSPF configuration mode, where settings like area assignments and router IDs are defined.

Additionally, access control lists (ACLs) can be configured on routers to filter traffic based on criteria like source and destination IP addresses, port numbers, and protocols. ACLs provide a layer of security and control over the traffic entering or leaving a network.

Switches, on the other hand, operate at the data link layer (Layer 2) of the OSI model and are responsible for forwarding frames within a local area network (LAN). Unlike routers, which make routing decisions based on IP addresses, switches use MAC (Media Access Control) addresses to determine the destination of frames within a LAN.

Configuring switches involves tasks such as assigning VLANs (Virtual Local Area Networks) to switch ports, creating trunk links between switches to carry multiple VLANs, and implementing spanning tree protocols to prevent network loops.

For instance, to assign a VLAN to a switch port, administrators use commands like "switchport access vlan" in the interface configuration mode. To create a trunk link between switches and allow the passage of multiple VLANs, the "switchport mode trunk" command is used. Spanning tree protocols like Rapid Spanning Tree Protocol (RSTP) or Multiple Spanning Tree Protocol (MSTP) can be configured to provide redundancy and loop prevention within the network.

In addition to configuring individual devices, network administrators must consider security measures to protect routers and switches from unauthorized access. This includes configuring secure passwords, enabling login banners, and implementing features like SSH (Secure Shell) for secure remote access.

Furthermore, device management and monitoring are essential aspects of router and switch configuration. Network administrators often use network management tools and protocols such as SNMP (Simple Network Management Protocol) to gather information about the status and performance of network devices. SNMP enables the monitoring of device parameters like CPU utilization, memory usage, and interface statistics.

To enhance network resilience and fault tolerance, administrators configure features like High Availability (HA) on routers and switches. HA mechanisms, such as Hot Standby Router Protocol (HSRP) or Virtual Router Redundancy Protocol (VRRP), ensure that if one router or switch fails, another can seamlessly take over to maintain network continuity.

Moreover, Quality of Service (QoS) configuration is vital for routers and switches to prioritize certain types of traffic over others, ensuring that critical applications receive the necessary bandwidth and low latency. QoS settings include defining traffic classes, assigning priorities, and implementing traffic shaping and policing policies.

When deploying routers and switches, network administrators should also consider network design principles, such as choosing the appropriate routing and switching technologies for the organization's needs. Factors like scalability, redundancy, and performance requirements influence the selection of router and switch models and configurations.

In a complex network environment, administrators may deploy routing protocols like BGP (Border Gateway Protocol) for internet connectivity, or MPLS (Multiprotocol Label Switching) to optimize traffic flow across wide-area networks (WANs). Each of these technologies requires specific configurations to operate effectively and efficiently.

Furthermore, cloud integration and Software-Defined Networking (SDN) have introduced new considerations for configuring routers and switches. SDN controllers centralize network management and allow administrators to dynamically adjust network behavior through software rather than manually configuring individual devices. Integrating cloud services often involves configuring Virtual Private Clouds (VPCs) or Virtual Networks (VNets) and establishing secure VPN connections to the cloud infrastructure.

In summary, configuring routers and switches is a crucial responsibility for network administrators, and it involves a wide range of tasks and considerations. Whether it's routing decisions, VLAN assignments, security settings, or network monitoring, meticulous configuration ensures that these devices perform optimally and provide the connectivity and services required by modern networks. With the ever-evolving landscape of networking technologies and the growing complexity of network environments, the role of configuring routers and switches remains essential for maintaining a robust and efficient network infrastructure.

Network Address Translation (NAT) is a fundamental networking technique that plays a crucial role in allowing multiple devices within a private network to share a single public IP address for internet communication. NAT serves as a bridge between the private network and the public internet, facilitating the secure and efficient exchange of data while conserving IP address resources.

The concept of NAT emerged due to the limited availability of IPv4 addresses. IPv4, with its 32-bit address space, can only provide a finite number of unique IP addresses, which became a significant concern as the internet grew in popularity. NAT was developed to address this scarcity issue by enabling the reuse of a single public IP address across many private devices.

The primary purpose of NAT is to hide the internal structure of a private network from external networks, such as the internet. In a typical NAT scenario, a private network consists of multiple devices, such as computers, smartphones, and IoT devices, each with its own private IP address. These private IP addresses are usually from reserved address ranges, such as 192.168.1.0/24 or 10.0.0.0/8, which are not routable on the public internet.

When a device within the private network initiates an outgoing connection to a server on the internet, NAT comes into play. The NAT device, often a router or firewall, acts as an intermediary. It assigns a unique port number to the outgoing traffic and modifies the source IP address of the packet to be the public IP address of the NAT device.

This process is known as "source NAT" or "SNAT." It allows multiple private devices to share the same public IP address by using different source port numbers to keep track of the connections. The NAT device maintains a translation table that maps the private IP address and port to the corresponding public IP address and port.

For example, if a private device with the IP address 192.168.1.2 initiates an HTTP request to a web server on the internet, the NAT device assigns a unique source port and modifies the packet's source IP address to the public IP address. The translation table records this mapping, enabling the NAT device to correctly route responses from the web server back to the originating private device.

To illustrate this concept further, consider the following CLI command used on a Cisco router to configure NAT:

scssCopy code

Router(config)# ip nat inside source static tcp 192.168.1.2 80 203.0.113.1 80

In this command, we are configuring static NAT to map the private IP address 192.168.1.2 on port 80 to the public IP address 203.0.113.1 on port 80. This means that any incoming traffic to the public IP address 203.0.113.1 on port

80 will be redirected to the private device with the IP address 192.168.1.2.

NAT can also be employed for incoming traffic, which is known as "destination NAT" or "DNAT." In this case, the NAT device receives incoming packets destined for its public IP address and port, and it translates the destination IP address and port to the appropriate private device within the network.

For example, if a web server in the private network with the IP address 192.168.1.10 needs to be accessible from the internet, DNAT can be configured on the NAT device to forward incoming traffic to this server. The NAT device maintains a translation table to keep track of the mappings between the public IP address and port and the private IP address and port.

Here is an example of a Cisco CLI command to configure DNAT:

scssCopy code

```
Router(config)# ip nat inside source static tcp 192.168.1.10 80 interface GigabitEthernet0/0 80
```

In this command, we are configuring static NAT to map incoming traffic on port 80 of the NAT device's public interface (GigabitEthernet0/0) to the private web server with the IP address 192.168.1.10 on port 80.

NAT provides several benefits, including IP address conservation, security, and network management. By allowing multiple private devices to share a single public IP address, NAT helps organizations make the most of their limited IPv4 address space. Additionally, NAT acts as a natural firewall, as it hides the internal network structure from external threats by modifying source and destination IP addresses.

Network administrators often deploy NAT to enhance network security and simplify internal network design. It allows them to consolidate public-facing services behind a single public IP address, reducing the exposure of internal devices to the internet. NAT also simplifies network management by centralizing the control of IP address assignments and routing.

However, there are some limitations to NAT. It can introduce complications for certain network protocols and applications that embed IP addresses within the data payload of packets, making them resistant to translation. Additionally, NAT can potentially hinder end-to-end connectivity and limit the ability to host certain services on private devices.

In summary, Network Address Translation (NAT) is a critical networking technique that addresses the challenges posed by the limited availability of IPv4 addresses. It enables multiple private devices to share a single public IP address for internet communication while maintaining security and efficient data exchange. NAT plays a central role in modern network design and is a valuable tool for network administrators in conserving IP addresses and enhancing network security.

## Chapter 5: Introduction to Routing

In the world of computer networking, routing is a fundamental process that dictates how data packets are directed from one network device to another. Within routing, there are two primary methods: static routing and dynamic routing, each with its advantages and disadvantages.

Static routing is a routing method where network administrators manually configure the routes that data packets should follow within a network. In this approach, administrators define the path or next-hop for data packets for specific destinations, creating a static route table.

Static routing is typically straightforward to set up and maintain since administrators have complete control over the routing decisions. They specify the exact routes data should take, making it easy to predict and troubleshoot network behavior. This predictability can be advantageous in small and stable network environments where changes in network topology are infrequent.

One common use case for static routing is in small office or home networks (SOHO) with a few devices, such as routers, connecting to the internet. Network administrators can configure static routes to direct traffic between the local network and the internet gateway.

To configure a static route on a Cisco router, for instance, the following command can be used:

arduinoCopy code

```
Router(config)#   ip   route   <destination_network> <subnet_mask> <next_hop_ip>
```

In this command, **<destination_network>** represents the network or subnet to which the static route applies,

**<subnet_mask>** specifies the subnet mask, and **<next_hop_ip>** indicates the next-hop router's IP address.

Static routing offers simplicity and low overhead since routers do not exchange routing information with other devices. This can make static routing more resource-efficient and suitable for devices with limited processing power and memory, such as older routers.

However, static routing has several limitations. One significant drawback is its lack of adaptability to changes in network topology. In dynamic network environments where devices frequently come online or go offline, or where network links may fail or be restored, static routes can become outdated and inefficient. Network administrators must manually update the route tables, which can be time-consuming and error-prone.

Moreover, in large and complex networks, managing static routes becomes challenging, as the number of routes to configure and maintain can become overwhelming. The risk of misconfigurations or route conflicts also increases, potentially leading to network disruptions.

Dynamic routing, on the other hand, automates the process of route determination by allowing routers to exchange routing information and make real-time decisions based on network conditions. Dynamic routing protocols enable routers to communicate with each other, share routing updates, and adapt to changes in the network dynamically.

One of the most widely used dynamic routing protocols is the Routing Information Protocol (RIP). RIP routers periodically broadcast routing updates to their neighboring routers, allowing them to learn about available routes and make routing decisions based on metrics like hop count. Cisco routers can be configured to use RIP with commands like:

arduinoCopy code

Router(config)# router rip  Router(config-router)# network <network_address>

In this example, the **network** command specifies the network address to include in RIP routing updates.

Dynamic routing offers several advantages, particularly in large and dynamic networks. It adapts to changes in network topology automatically, which means that routers can adjust their routing tables in real time as network conditions evolve. This adaptability is essential for networks with varying traffic loads, link failures, or frequent device mobility.

Dynamic routing protocols can also calculate optimal routes based on various metrics, such as bandwidth, delay, or cost, depending on the protocol. This results in more efficient use of network resources and better performance.

Furthermore, dynamic routing protocols are inherently scalable. They can handle networks with hundreds or even thousands of routers and devices, making them suitable for enterprise-level networks and service providers.

However, dynamic routing does come with some complexities. Configuration and management can be more involved, and routers must exchange routing updates, consuming network bandwidth and router processing power. In large networks, administrators need to monitor and fine-tune the dynamic routing protocols to ensure optimal performance and stability.

Another consideration is security. Dynamic routing protocols may be vulnerable to attacks if not properly secured. To mitigate security risks, network administrators can implement authentication mechanisms and access controls for routing updates.

Choosing between static routing and dynamic routing depends on the specific needs and characteristics of the network. Small and stable networks with simple requirements may benefit from the simplicity of static routing. In contrast, dynamic routing is well-suited for larger, more complex networks that require adaptability, scalability, and efficient resource utilization.

It's also common to use a combination of both static and dynamic routing in the same network. For example, organizations might use static routes for essential network infrastructure, such as the default route to the internet gateway, while employing dynamic routing for internal network segments that experience frequent changes.

In summary, static routing and dynamic routing are two fundamental approaches to routing in computer networks, each with its advantages and trade-offs. Network administrators must carefully evaluate their network requirements, size, stability, and complexity to determine which routing method or combination of methods best meets their needs. Whether opting for the simplicity of static routing or the adaptability of dynamic routing, routing remains a cornerstone of modern networking, guiding the flow of data across interconnected devices and networks.

Routing protocols are the intelligence behind the way data packets navigate networks, determining the optimal paths for information to travel from source to destination. In the world of computer networking, routing protocols are essential components that enable routers to make informed decisions about where to forward data. These protocols play a vital role in ensuring that data arrives at its intended destination efficiently and reliably.

Routing protocols fall into two broad categories: interior routing protocols (IRPs) and exterior routing protocols (ERPs). IRPs are used within autonomous systems or networks, while ERPs connect multiple autonomous systems or networks together. The choice of routing protocol depends on the network's size, complexity, and requirements.

Within interior routing protocols, there are two primary categories: distance-vector routing protocols and link-state routing protocols. Distance-vector protocols, such as Routing Information Protocol (RIP) and Interior Gateway Routing Protocol (IGRP), operate based on hop count and periodically exchange routing tables with neighboring routers. These protocols are simple to configure but may not scale well in large or complex networks due to their limited understanding of network topology.

For instance, RIP, a distance-vector protocol, can be configured on a Cisco router with the following command: arduinoCopy code

```
Router(config)# router rip  Router(config-router)# network <network_address>
```

Link-state routing protocols, on the other hand, focus on maintaining a detailed and up-to-date view of the entire network's topology. They exchange link-state advertisements (LSAs) to build a comprehensive picture of network routes. Notable link-state protocols include Open Shortest Path First (OSPF) and Intermediate System to Intermediate System (IS-IS).

Here is an example of configuring OSPF on a Cisco router: arduinoCopy code

```
Router(config)# router ospf <process_id>  Router(config-router)# network <network_address> <wildcard_mask> area <area_id>
```

Exterior routing protocols, such as Border Gateway Protocol (BGP), play a critical role in connecting autonomous systems on the global internet. BGP is a path vector protocol that focuses on exchanging routing information between different autonomous systems (ASes) to determine the best path for data to travel across the internet.

BGP configuration on a router involves specifying neighbor relationships and defining routing policies. An example of BGP configuration on a Cisco router might include:

arduinoCopy code

```
Router(config)# router bgp <AS_number> Router(config-router)# neighbor <neighbor_ip> remote-as <neighbor_AS>
```

In addition to distance-vector, link-state, and path vector routing protocols, there are also hybrid routing protocols, such as Enhanced Interior Gateway Routing Protocol (EIGRP), which combines elements of both distance-vector and link-state protocols. EIGRP, developed by Cisco, is known for its efficiency and rapid convergence, making it suitable for large enterprise networks.

Configuring EIGRP on a Cisco router involves defining autonomous system settings and network advertisements:

arduinoCopy code

```
Router(config)# router eigrp <AS_number> Router(config-router)# network <network_address>
```

Routing protocols operate based on algorithms and metrics to determine the best paths for data packets. Metrics can include factors like hop count, bandwidth, delay, and cost. Each routing protocol uses its specific algorithm to calculate the optimal routes based on these metrics.

Moreover, routers exchange routing information through routing updates, which are messages containing details about network routes. These updates help routers build and maintain their routing tables. The frequency and method of exchanging updates vary among routing protocols.

Some routing protocols are classful, while others are classless. Classful protocols do not transmit subnet mask information in their routing updates, relying on the default subnet masks associated with IP address classes. Classless protocols, on the other hand, include subnet mask information in their updates, allowing for more precise route advertisements.

In addition to the protocol type, routing protocols can be categorized as either static or dynamic. Static routing requires administrators to manually configure routing tables, specifying the exact routes data should follow. Dynamic routing, in contrast, enables routers to exchange routing information and adapt to changes in the network topology automatically.

Routing protocols also employ administrative distance (AD) values to determine the trustworthiness of routing information from various sources. The lower the AD value, the more trusted the route. If a router receives conflicting routing information, it will choose the route with the lowest AD value.

Redistribution is another essential concept in routing protocols, particularly in networks that use multiple routing protocols. Redistribution allows routers to share routing information between different protocols, enabling seamless communication within the network.

Furthermore, routing protocols have mechanisms for loop prevention and loop detection. These mechanisms ensure that data packets do not endlessly circulate within the network and that routing loops are promptly resolved to maintain network stability.

The choice of which routing protocol to use depends on various factors, including the network's size, complexity, performance requirements, and compatibility with existing equipment. Network administrators must carefully evaluate their network's needs and constraints to select the most appropriate routing protocol or combination of protocols.

Finally, routing protocols play a central role in maintaining the connectivity and reliability of modern computer networks. They are a foundational element of the internet, enterprise networks, and service provider networks, ensuring that data travels efficiently and accurately to its intended destinations. As networking technology continues to evolve, routing protocols will continue to adapt and play a vital role in shaping the future of network communication.

## Chapter 6: Transport Layer Protocols: TCP and UDP

Transmission Control Protocol (TCP) is a core protocol of the internet, serving as a reliable and connection-oriented method for delivering data between devices across networks. TCP is one of the two main protocols within the TCP/IP suite, with the other being Internet Protocol (IP), and together they form the foundation of internet communication.

At its core, TCP is designed to ensure that data transmitted from one device reaches its destination accurately, completely, and in the correct order. To achieve this, TCP provides a set of features and mechanisms that address common issues that can occur during data transmission, such as data loss, data corruption, and out-of-order delivery.

One of the key features of TCP is its reliability. When two devices establish a TCP connection, they exchange a series of control messages to set up the connection and negotiate various parameters. Once the connection is established, data can be sent with the assurance that it will be reliably delivered to the other end.

The reliability of TCP is achieved through several mechanisms, including acknowledgment (ACK) packets, sequence numbers, and retransmission. When a device receives a TCP segment, it sends an acknowledgment packet back to the sender to confirm that it received the data successfully. If the sender does not receive an acknowledgment within a certain time frame, it assumes that the data was lost and retransmits it.

Sequence numbers play a crucial role in ensuring that data is delivered in the correct order. Each segment of data sent over a TCP connection is assigned a sequence number, allowing the receiver to reassemble the data in the correct order. If segments arrive out of order, the receiver can request retransmission of the missing segments based on their sequence numbers.

Another important aspect of TCP is flow control. Flow control mechanisms prevent a sender from overwhelming a receiver with data. In TCP, this is achieved through a sliding window approach. The receiver advertises a window size to the sender, indicating how much data it can accept before needing further acknowledgment. This window size can vary dynamically based on the receiver's available buffer space.

To illustrate TCP's reliability and flow control mechanisms, let's consider a scenario where a user is downloading a large file from a web server. As the file is transmitted in segments over the internet, each segment is acknowledged by the user's device. If a segment is lost or corrupted in transit, the user's device requests retransmission of that specific segment, ensuring the complete and accurate delivery of the file.

Additionally, TCP incorporates congestion control mechanisms to prevent network congestion and ensure fair bandwidth utilization. Congestion control algorithms, such as TCP Tahoe and TCP Reno, adjust the sending rate based on network conditions. If congestion is detected, the sender reduces its sending rate to alleviate network congestion and maintain network stability.

Configuring and monitoring TCP behavior on network devices often involves the use of command-line interfaces (CLIs) or graphical user interfaces (GUIs). For example, network administrators can adjust TCP-related parameters, such as maximum segment size (MSS) or congestion control algorithms, on routers and switches using CLIs.

Furthermore, TCP includes support for various options that can be negotiated during the connection establishment phase. These options can include Maximum Segment Size (MSS), Window Scale, Selective Acknowledgment (SACK), and Timestamps. These options enhance the protocol's flexibility and performance based on the specific needs of the application and network.

In addition to its role in internet communication, TCP is widely used in various applications and protocols. Web browsing, email, file transfer (e.g., FTP), and remote login (e.g., SSH) are just a few examples of applications that rely on TCP for reliable data delivery.

While TCP offers many advantages, it is not suitable for all scenarios. Real-time applications, such as voice and video conferencing, may require low-latency communication and are often better served by the User Datagram Protocol (UDP), which sacrifices reliability for reduced latency.

In summary, Transmission Control Protocol (TCP) is a cornerstone of internet communication, providing reliable, connection-oriented data delivery between devices across networks. TCP's mechanisms for reliability, flow control, and congestion control ensure the accurate and efficient transmission of data. Understanding TCP is essential for network administrators, as it forms the basis for a wide range of internet applications and services. Whether configuring network devices or troubleshooting connectivity issues, a solid grasp of TCP is invaluable in the world of networking.

User Datagram Protocol (UDP) is another core protocol in the TCP/IP suite, but it differs significantly from Transmission Control Protocol (TCP) in terms of its characteristics and use cases. UDP is a connectionless, lightweight protocol that provides a minimalistic approach to data transmission, offering advantages in specific scenarios where speed and simplicity are prioritized over reliability.

UDP is often referred to as a "best-effort" protocol because it does not guarantee the reliable delivery of data packets. Unlike TCP, UDP does not establish a connection, perform handshakes, or maintain state information about data transmission. Instead, it simply encapsulates data into packets and sends them to the destination without acknowledgment or error recovery mechanisms.

One of the primary characteristics of UDP is its low overhead. Because it lacks the complex mechanisms of TCP for managing connections and ensuring reliability, UDP header overhead is minimal, consisting of only source and destination port numbers, length, and a checksum field. This efficiency makes UDP well-suited for applications where reducing overhead and latency are critical.

One common use case for UDP is real-time communication applications, such as voice over IP (VoIP) and video conferencing. In these applications, low latency and fast transmission of audio and video data are essential. UDP's lightweight nature allows it to transmit real-time media packets quickly, but it does not provide retransmission of lost packets, which means that occasional packet loss may occur.

For example, in VoIP applications, voice data is divided into small packets and sent as UDP datagrams. While this approach minimizes latency, it can result in occasional audio dropouts if some packets are lost during transmission. VoIP applications typically incorporate mechanisms to mitigate packet loss, such as jitter buffers and forward error correction (FEC).

Another significant use case for UDP is in Domain Name System (DNS) communication. DNS resolves domain names to IP addresses and operates on UDP port 53 by default. DNS queries and responses are typically small and can be quickly transmitted using UDP, which is suitable for the nature of

DNS requests, where low overhead and fast responses are desired.

Configuring UDP for DNS involves specifying the UDP transport protocol and port number. In a Cisco router, for example, DNS can be configured with the following commands:

arduinoCopy code

```
Router(config)#   ip   name-server   <DNS_server_IP>
Router(config)# ip domain-lookup
```

In these commands, **<DNS_server_IP>** represents the IP address of the DNS server to be used for name resolution.

UDP is also commonly used for broadcasting and multicasting. Broadcasting involves sending data packets to all devices on a network segment, while multicasting targets a specific group of devices interested in receiving the data. Both techniques can be employed for various purposes, such as network discovery and content distribution.

UDP's simplicity makes it suitable for applications that can tolerate occasional data loss, such as online gaming. In online gaming, rapid transmission of player positions and actions is crucial for maintaining a responsive gaming experience. While UDP may result in occasional packet loss or out-of-order delivery, game developers often implement techniques like client-side prediction and server reconciliation to compensate for these limitations.

Moreover, UDP can be advantageous in scenarios where network resources are limited or constrained. For example, in Internet of Things (IoT) devices or embedded systems with low processing power and memory, UDP's minimal overhead makes it a practical choice for transmitting sensor data or control commands.

UDP is also suitable for scenarios where the overhead of establishing and maintaining a TCP connection is unnecessary. For instance, in situations where a device periodically sends status updates or telemetry data to a central server, UDP can efficiently transmit this information without the overhead associated with TCP's connection management.

However, it's essential to recognize that UDP's lack of reliability means that applications built on UDP must handle error detection and recovery independently. This can involve implementing custom mechanisms for detecting missing or out-of-order packets and deciding how to respond to such events.

In summary, User Datagram Protocol (UDP) is a connectionless and lightweight protocol that prioritizes speed and simplicity over reliability. UDP's characteristics make it well-suited for real-time communication, DNS resolution, broadcasting, multicasting, online gaming, and resource-constrained devices. While UDP may not guarantee the reliable delivery of data, it offers advantages in scenarios where low overhead, minimal latency, and efficient data transmission are paramount. Understanding the use cases and limitations of UDP is essential for network architects and application developers as they design and implement systems that leverage this protocol for specific purposes.

## Chapter 7: DNS and DHCP Fundamentals

Domain Name System (DNS) is a fundamental technology that plays a crucial role in translating human-readable domain names into machine-readable IP addresses, allowing devices to locate and communicate with each other on the internet.

The process of DNS resolution is an essential part of how the internet functions, as it enables users to access websites, send emails, and perform various online activities by simply entering domain names into their web browsers or applications.

To understand how DNS resolves domain names, we need to explore the various components and steps involved in the DNS resolution process.

At the heart of the DNS system are DNS servers, which are responsible for storing and managing DNS records. DNS servers fall into different categories, including recursive resolvers, authoritative servers, and root servers, each with specific roles in the DNS resolution process.

When a user enters a domain name (e.g., www.example.com) into a web browser's address bar, the DNS resolution process begins. The user's device typically starts by querying a local DNS resolver, often provided by the internet service provider (ISP) or a DNS resolver service.

The local DNS resolver checks its cache to see if it has a recent record of the requested domain name and its corresponding IP address. If the record is found and still valid, the resolver can immediately provide the IP address to the user's device, allowing it to establish a connection to the target server.

However, if the local DNS resolver does not have a cached record or if the cached record has expired, it initiates a recursive DNS query. This query is the first step in the DNS resolution process, and it seeks to find the IP address associated with the requested domain name.

The recursive DNS query is sent to a recursive DNS resolver, which is a specialized DNS server designed to handle such queries. The recursive resolver plays a critical role in the DNS resolution process by taking on the responsibility of finding the IP address of the requested domain.

Upon receiving the recursive DNS query, the recursive resolver checks its own cache for a valid record of the domain name. If the record is present and up-to-date, the resolver returns the IP address to the local DNS resolver, which, in turn, provides it to the user's device.

If the recursive resolver does not have a cached record for the domain name or if the cached record has expired, it must traverse the DNS hierarchy to find the authoritative DNS server for the target domain.

This traversal begins at the root DNS servers, which are a set of highly distributed and redundant servers worldwide. The root DNS servers are responsible for the highest level of the DNS hierarchy and contain information about the authoritative DNS servers for top-level domains (TLDs).

The recursive resolver sends a query to a root DNS server, asking for information about the authoritative DNS server responsible for the TLD of the requested domain name (e.g., ".com" for www.example.com).

The root DNS server responds with a referral, indicating the IP address of the authoritative DNS server for the TLD. The recursive resolver then queries the TLD authoritative DNS server to obtain information about the authoritative DNS server for the specific domain name (e.g., "example.com" for www.example.com).

Once the recursive resolver has obtained the IP address of the authoritative DNS server for the domain name, it sends a query to this authoritative DNS server, requesting the A (Address) record, which contains the IP address associated with the domain.

The authoritative DNS server responds to the query by providing the requested A record, which contains the IP address of the target server for the domain name.

With the IP address in hand, the recursive resolver sends the information back to the local DNS resolver, which, in turn, delivers it to the user's device.

Armed with the IP address, the user's device can now establish a connection to the target server associated with the domain name. This connection enables the user to access the desired website or service on the internet.

In summary, the DNS resolution process involves a series of steps that begin with the user's device querying a local DNS resolver. If the resolver does not have a cached record, it initiates a recursive DNS query that traverses the DNS hierarchy, starting with the root DNS servers and progressing to the authoritative DNS servers for the target domain. Once the IP address is obtained, it is returned to the user's device, enabling it to establish a connection to the desired server. DNS is a fundamental technology that underpins internet communication, making it possible for users to navigate the web and access online resources using human-readable domain names. Understanding the DNS resolution process is essential for anyone working with internet technologies, as it forms the foundation of how domain names are translated into IP addresses.

The Dynamic Host Configuration Protocol (DHCP) lease process is a fundamental mechanism used in computer networking to assign IP addresses dynamically to devices on a network, such as computers, smartphones, and IoT devices.

This process enables the efficient allocation of IP addresses from a central DHCP server, simplifying network administration and ensuring that devices have the necessary network configuration to communicate over the network.

To understand the DHCP lease process, we need to explore the series of steps that occur when a device requests an IP address and associated network configuration through DHCP.

The process begins when a device, often referred to as the DHCP client, connects to a network and requires an IP address to participate in network communication. The client sends a DHCP request to the local network, seeking an available IP address and related configuration parameters.

The DHCP request is typically broadcast to the local subnet, making it visible to all DHCP servers within that subnet. This broadcast is a DHCPDISCOVER message, indicating that the client is actively seeking a DHCP server to fulfill its IP address request.

Upon receiving the DHCPDISCOVER message, one or more DHCP servers on the local subnet may respond. These servers listen for DHCP requests and can offer IP addresses and related configuration parameters to clients. In the response to the DHCPDISCOVER message, a DHCP server sends a DHCPOFFER message, providing the client with a proposed IP address and associated network settings.

The DHCPOFFER message includes an IP address that the server intends to lease to the client, along with subnet mask information, gateway (router) address, DNS server addresses, and lease duration. The lease duration specifies how long the client can use the assigned IP address and configuration settings.

Upon receiving one or more DHCPOFFER messages from available DHCP servers, the client evaluates the offers and selects one of the proposed IP addresses and configurations. It sends a DHCPREQUEST message, specifying the server's offer that it has chosen. This message indicates the client's intention to accept the lease offered by a particular DHCP server.

At this point, multiple DHCP servers may have received the client's DHCPREQUEST message and will process it accordingly. To avoid conflicts and ensure that only one server leases the IP address to the client, the DHCP servers engage in a communication process called DHCP server selection.

The DHCP servers that received the DHCPREQUEST message from the client communicate with each other to determine which one should fulfill the lease request. This communication helps prevent IP address conflicts and ensures that only one server assigns the IP address.

Once the DHCP servers agree on which server should fulfill the lease, the chosen server sends a DHCPACK message to the client. The DHCPACK message confirms that the client has been granted the requested IP address and associated configuration parameters.

The DHCPACK message also includes the lease duration, specifying the time period during which the client is allowed to use the assigned IP address. This lease duration is essential because DHCP leases are not permanent; they have a limited lifespan.

The client receives the DHCPACK message and acknowledges it with a DHCPACKNOWLEDGE message, confirming that it has accepted the lease. At this point, the client has successfully obtained an IP address and network configuration through DHCP.

Throughout the lease duration, the client can use the assigned IP address to communicate on the network. It can send and receive data, access network resources, and perform various network-related tasks.

As the lease expiration time approaches, the client can proactively request a lease renewal to continue using the IP address without interruption. To request a lease renewal, the client sends a DHCPREQUEST message to the DHCP server that originally granted the lease. The server can then extend the lease duration or assign a new lease, allowing the client to maintain its network connectivity.

If, for any reason, the client no longer requires the leased IP address or experiences network disconnection, it can send a DHCPRELEASE message to the DHCP server to release the IP address back to the pool of available addresses. Releasing the IP address is a good practice, as it helps manage IP address allocation efficiently.

Network administrators often use command-line interfaces (CLIs) or graphical user interfaces (GUIs) to configure and manage DHCP servers. Configuration involves specifying IP address pools, lease durations, and various network settings, such as subnet masks, gateway addresses, and DNS server information.

The DHCP lease process is a dynamic and essential component of network management, allowing devices to obtain IP addresses and network configurations seamlessly. It simplifies network administration, reduces the risk of IP address conflicts, and ensures efficient utilization of available IP addresses. Understanding the DHCP lease process is crucial for network administrators and anyone involved in managing IP address allocation in computer networks.

## Chapter 8: Common Network Services and Applications

File Transfer Protocols, such as FTP (File Transfer Protocol) and SFTP (Secure File Transfer Protocol), are essential tools for transferring files between computers and servers over a network.

FTP, one of the earliest file transfer protocols, provides a simple and efficient way to upload and download files between a client and a server.

Using FTP often involves the command-line interface or graphical FTP clients, where users enter FTP commands to initiate file transfers.

To connect to an FTP server using the command line, you can use the "ftp" command followed by the server's hostname or IP address, like this:

Copy code

```
ftp server.example.com
```

Upon successful connection, you need to log in with valid credentials, typically a username and password provided by the FTP server administrator.

To upload a file from your local machine to the FTP server, you use the "put" command followed by the local file's name, like this:

arduinoCopy code

```
put myfile.txt
```

Conversely, to download a file from the FTP server to your local machine, you use the "get" command followed by the remote file's name, like this:

arduinoCopy code

```
get remotefile.txt
```

FTP is a straightforward and widely supported protocol, making it suitable for basic file transfers.

However, it has some limitations, particularly concerning security. FTP transfers data and credentials in plain text, making it vulnerable to eavesdropping and unauthorized access.

To address these security concerns, Secure File Transfer Protocol (SFTP) was developed as a secure alternative to FTP.

SFTP operates over a secure channel, typically using SSH (Secure Shell) for authentication and encryption, ensuring the confidentiality and integrity of data in transit.

To connect to an SFTP server using the command line, you can use the "sftp" command followed by the server's hostname or IP address, just like FTP:

Copy code

sftp server.example.com

Once connected, you log in using your SFTP username and password or SSH keys if configured for key-based authentication.

SFTP commands are similar to those of FTP but operate within a secure environment, protecting data and credentials from interception.

For example, to upload a file using SFTP, you can use the "put" command:

arduinoCopy code

put myfile.txt

And to download a file:

arduinoCopy code

get remotefile.txt

SFTP is widely used in secure file transfer scenarios, such as remote backups, file synchronization, and secure data exchanges.

While both FTP and SFTP serve the purpose of file transfer, they differ significantly in terms of security, capabilities, and use cases.

FTP is a legacy protocol that lacks robust security features, and its use is generally discouraged for sensitive data transfers over untrusted networks.

In contrast, SFTP offers strong encryption and authentication mechanisms, making it suitable for secure data exchange in various contexts, including business operations, web hosting, and server administration.

When choosing between FTP and SFTP, consider the security requirements of your file transfers and opt for SFTP when confidentiality and data integrity are paramount.

Furthermore, both FTP and SFTP can be used in automated file transfer workflows. You can script FTP or SFTP commands in batch files or use them in conjunction with tools like cron on Unix-like systems or Task Scheduler on Windows to schedule and automate file transfers at specified intervals.

For example, to automate an SFTP file upload using a script, you might create a shell script (e.g., upload.sh) containing the following commands:

bashCopy code

```
#!/bin/bash                    HOST='server.example.com'
USER='yourusername'    PASS='yourpassword'       sftp
$USER@$HOST <<EOF cd /remote/directory put localfile.txt
bye EOF
```

In this script, replace 'server.example.com,' 'yourusername,' and 'yourpassword' with your SFTP server details, and specify the remote directory and local file you want to transfer.

Running the script with a command like "./upload.sh" would automate the secure file upload process.

FTP and SFTP are versatile tools for file transfers, with their own strengths and weaknesses.

FTP is simple and suitable for basic file transfers but lacks security features, while SFTP offers robust security but requires more complex setup and configuration.

The choice between them depends on your specific requirements and the level of security needed for your file transfer operations.

Whether you're using FTP or SFTP, understanding how to use these protocols effectively and securely is essential for managing and exchanging files in a networked environment.

Email protocols, such as SMTP (Simple Mail Transfer Protocol) and POP3 (Post Office Protocol version 3), are the backbone of modern email communication, enabling the exchange of messages between email clients and servers.

SMTP, in particular, is responsible for sending outgoing emails, while POP3 facilitates the retrieval of emails from a mail server to a client device.

SMTP plays a vital role in the process of sending emails by ensuring that messages are routed and delivered to the intended recipients.

SMTP operates on the client-server model, where the email client, such as Microsoft Outlook or Mozilla Thunderbird, communicates with an SMTP server to transmit outgoing messages.

To send an email using SMTP from a command-line interface, you can use a command like "telnet" to connect to the SMTP server:

Copy code

```
telnet smtp.example.com 25
```

This command establishes a connection to the SMTP server at "smtp.example.com" on port 25, which is the default SMTP port.

Once connected, you interact with the SMTP server by issuing SMTP commands. For example, to start an SMTP session, you can use the "EHLO" (Extended Hello) command:

Copy code

EHLO example.com

After the session is established, you can provide sender and recipient information, the subject, and the body of the email using SMTP commands.

Once all necessary information is provided, the email is sent to the SMTP server for further processing and delivery to the recipient's email server.

SMTP is a robust and widely adopted protocol for sending emails, providing reliability and flexibility for email communication.

On the other hand, POP3 focuses on the retrieval of emails from a mail server to a client device.

POP3 operates over TCP/IP and uses port 110 by default for unencrypted connections, or port 995 for encrypted connections using SSL/TLS.

To retrieve emails from a POP3 server using a command-line interface, you can use a utility like "telnet" or "openssl" for encrypted connections:

For unencrypted POP3 connections:

Copy code

telnet pop.example.com 110

For encrypted POP3 connections using OpenSSL:

arduinoCopy code

openssl s_client -connect pop.example.com:995

Once connected, you interact with the POP3 server by issuing POP3 commands to perform actions such as retrieving emails, deleting emails, or listing emails in your mailbox.

For example, to authenticate and retrieve emails from a POP3 server, you can use commands like "USER," "PASS," "LIST," and "RETR":

sqlCopy code

USER your_username PASS your_password LIST RETR 1

These commands allow you to log in with your username and password, list the emails available in your mailbox, and retrieve a specific email by its message number.

POP3 is a simple protocol designed for downloading emails to a local client device, making it suitable for scenarios where users want to keep a local copy of their emails.

However, one limitation of POP3 is that it typically downloads emails to a single client, making it less suitable for situations where multiple devices need access to the same email mailbox.

To address this limitation, another email protocol called IMAP (Internet Message Access Protocol) was developed. IMAP allows multiple devices to synchronize and access the same mailbox while keeping emails stored on the server.

The choice between POP3 and IMAP depends on your specific email requirements and how you prefer to manage your emails.

Email clients and servers often support both POP3 and IMAP, allowing users to select the protocol that best suits their needs.

In summary, SMTP and POP3 are fundamental email protocols that play distinct roles in the process of sending and receiving emails.

SMTP facilitates the sending of outgoing emails from a client to a server, ensuring that messages are routed and delivered to the recipients' email servers.

POP3, on the other hand, enables users to retrieve emails from a server to their client devices, making it convenient for keeping local copies of emails.

Understanding how these email protocols work and when to use them is crucial for effectively managing and communicating through email systems.

## Chapter 9: Network Security Basics

Firewall technologies are critical components of network security, serving as barriers between trusted internal networks and potentially untrusted external networks, such as the internet.

Firewalls are designed to monitor, filter, and control incoming and outgoing network traffic based on predefined security rules and policies.

One of the most common types of firewalls is the packet-filtering firewall, which examines data packets as they pass through the firewall and makes decisions about whether to allow or block them based on specific criteria.

Packet-filtering firewalls can be implemented in various ways, including through hardware appliances or software installed on network devices.

For example, on a Linux system, you can use the "iptables" command to configure packet filtering rules:

cssCopy code

```
iptables -A INPUT -s 192.168.1.0/24 -p tcp --dport 80 -j ACCEPT
```

This command allows incoming TCP traffic on port 80 from the 192.168.1.0/24 subnet.

Packet-filtering firewalls are effective at blocking unauthorized traffic but may have limitations in handling more complex scenarios, such as application-layer attacks or deep packet inspection.

To address these limitations, next-generation firewalls (NGFWs) have emerged, offering advanced features like intrusion detection and prevention, application-layer filtering, and content filtering.

NGFWs are equipped to inspect traffic at the application layer, enabling them to identify and block specific applications or services, even if they operate on non-standard ports.

For instance, a NGFW can be configured to allow or block access to social media sites, instant messaging services, or file-sharing applications based on defined policies.

NGFWs also incorporate threat intelligence and signature-based detection mechanisms to identify and prevent known threats, such as malware, viruses, and exploits.

In addition to packet-filtering and NGFWs, stateful inspection firewalls provide another layer of security by maintaining a stateful table of active connections and evaluating packets in the context of established sessions.

This stateful approach helps prevent unauthorized access by ensuring that incoming packets are part of a legitimate and established session, reducing the risk of attacks like IP spoofing or session hijacking.

Configuring stateful inspection rules often involves specifying allowed inbound and outbound traffic based on the state of the connection, such as allowing outbound responses to established connections but blocking inbound unsolicited traffic.

Firewalls can also be deployed in various network architectures, including perimeter, host-based, and cloud-based configurations.

A perimeter firewall is typically placed at the boundary between an internal network and an external network, acting as the first line of defense against incoming threats.

Perimeter firewalls are often deployed in a demilitarized zone (DMZ) to filter traffic between the internal network and the internet while allowing specific services to be exposed to external users.

Host-based firewalls, on the other hand, are installed directly on individual devices, such as servers or workstations, to control traffic to and from that specific device.

Host-based firewalls are particularly useful for securing endpoint devices and can be customized to meet specific security requirements.

Cloud-based firewalls are designed to protect cloud resources and applications hosted on public or private cloud platforms.

These firewalls operate in a distributed manner, filtering traffic at multiple points across cloud environments, providing scalability and flexibility in securing cloud-based workloads.

Firewall technologies are continuously evolving to address emerging threats and adapt to changing network architectures.

Intrusion prevention systems (IPS), for example, are often integrated into firewalls to detect and block malicious activities in real-time, helping organizations respond to security incidents more effectively.

Web application firewalls (WAFs) are specialized firewalls designed to protect web applications from common web-based attacks, such as SQL injection and cross-site scripting (XSS).

To configure and manage advanced firewall features, network administrators often use dedicated management interfaces or command-line interfaces (CLIs) provided by firewall vendors.

For instance, the Cisco ASA firewall uses the "configure terminal" command to access the CLI configuration mode and configure firewall rules:
arduinoCopy code

configure terminal access-list outside_access_in permit tcp any host 203.0.113.1 eq 80

This command allows incoming TCP traffic on port 80 to the host with IP address 203.0.113.1.

Firewall technologies are a critical part of network security, providing essential protection against unauthorized access, threats, and attacks.

Understanding the different types of firewalls, their deployment options, and how to configure them is essential for network administrators and security professionals to maintain a secure network infrastructure.

As cyber threats continue to evolve, firewalls will remain a fundamental component of a comprehensive security strategy, helping organizations safeguard their digital assets and data.

Intrusion Detection and Prevention Systems (IDPS) are integral components of modern cybersecurity, serving as advanced sentinels that monitor network and system activities to detect and thwart potential security threats.

These systems play a crucial role in identifying suspicious or malicious behavior, helping organizations protect their digital assets and sensitive data from cyberattacks.

IDPS solutions come in various forms, each tailored to specific use cases and deployment scenarios, providing flexibility and adaptability in safeguarding network environments.

Network-based IDPS, for instance, operate at the network level, examining network traffic and packet data to identify anomalies or patterns indicative of malicious activity.

This type of IDPS can be deployed strategically at network chokepoints, such as firewalls or routers, to analyze incoming and outgoing traffic.

To configure a network-based IDPS, network administrators often use dedicated management interfaces or command-line interfaces (CLIs) provided by the IDPS vendor.

For example, the Suricata open-source IDPS offers a command-line interface for configuring and managing intrusion detection rules:

bashCopy code

```
suricata -c /etc/suricata/suricata.yaml -i eth0
```

This command starts Suricata on the "eth0" network interface using the configuration file "/etc/suricata/suricata.yaml."

Host-based IDPS, on the other hand, are deployed directly on individual hosts, such as servers or workstations, to monitor local system activities and detect intrusions.

Host-based IDPS solutions can identify suspicious processes, file modifications, or unauthorized access attempts on a per-host basis.

To illustrate, the OSSEC Host-based Intrusion Detection System uses a configuration file that allows users to specify rules for monitoring and alerting on host-based security events:

phpCopy code

```
<group name="syslog"> <group name=""> <rule id="1002" level="3">     <decoded_as>json</decoded_as>     <field name="log">authentication                failure;</field> <description>Authentication Failure</description> </rule> </group> </group>
```

In this example, a rule is defined to detect authentication failures in syslog messages, triggering an alert with a specified severity level.

IDPS systems rely on predefined signatures, rules, or behavioral analytics to detect potential threats.

For instance, signature-based IDPS use predefined patterns or signatures of known attacks, comparing them to observed network or system traffic to identify matches.

Behavioral-based IDPS, on the other hand, monitor for deviations from established baselines of normal behavior, triggering alerts when unusual activities are detected.

To enhance their effectiveness, many IDPS solutions incorporate threat intelligence feeds and regularly updated signature databases to identify the latest threats.

IDPS solutions not only detect intrusions but can also take preventive actions to stop or mitigate attacks in real-time.

Intrusion Prevention Systems (IPS), a subset of IDPS, go beyond detection by actively blocking or preventing malicious activities from compromising network resources.

For example, an IPS can block specific IP addresses or communication ports associated with malicious traffic, preventing further access or harm.

To configure an IPS, network administrators often use interfaces provided by the IPS vendor, defining rules and policies for blocking and preventing malicious traffic.

The following is an example of configuring a rule to block incoming traffic from a specific IP address range using the Snort IPS:

pythonCopy code

```
alert ip 192.168.1.0/24 any -> any any (msg:"Block traffic from IP range"; sid:100001;)
```

This Snort rule blocks all incoming traffic from the IP address range 192.168.1.0/24.

IDPS solutions are not limited to just network and host-based deployments; they can also be integrated into cloud environments to safeguard cloud resources and applications.

Cloud-based IDPS offer the flexibility to protect cloud workloads, data, and services from threats, with the advantage of scalability and centralized management.

Intrusion Detection and Prevention Systems can operate in a standalone fashion or as part of a broader security ecosystem, working in conjunction with firewalls, antivirus software, and security information and event management (SIEM) systems.

SIEM systems integrate security information from various sources, including IDPS alerts, to provide a centralized view of an organization's security posture and enable comprehensive threat analysis and response.

The effectiveness of an IDPS depends on the accuracy of its detection mechanisms, the timeliness of updates, and the ability to adapt to evolving threats.

Regular updates to signatures and behavioral analysis techniques are essential to keep the IDPS up-to-date with the latest threat intelligence.

In addition to detection and prevention capabilities, IDPS often provide reporting and alerting features, allowing security teams to investigate and respond to security incidents promptly. The alerts generated by an IDPS are typically classified based on their severity and relevance, enabling security analysts to prioritize their response efforts. IDPS solutions are not without challenges; false positives, where benign activities are mistakenly identified as threats, can lead to alert fatigue and decreased effectiveness.

To mitigate false positives, tuning and customization of IDPS rules and policies are often necessary, aligning them with the specific network environment and threat landscape.

Furthermore, IDPS deployment and operation require skilled security professionals who understand the nuances of network traffic and system behaviors, ensuring that the system is configured correctly and efficiently.

In summary, Intrusion Detection and Prevention Systems are essential components of modern cybersecurity, playing a vital role in identifying and mitigating security threats in network and host environments.

These systems are available in various forms, including network-based and host-based deployments, with the ability to operate in cloud environments.

IDPS solutions use a combination of signature-based and behavioral-based techniques to detect and prevent intrusions, and they often include features for alerting, reporting, and integration with broader security ecosystems. Maintaining an effective IDPS requires regular updates, tuning, and skilled security personnel to adapt to evolving threats and ensure accurate threat detection and response.

## Chapter 10: Troubleshooting TCP/IP Networks

Network troubleshooting is a fundamental skill for IT professionals, as it allows them to diagnose and resolve network issues efficiently, ensuring that networks run smoothly and provide reliable connectivity.

A structured network troubleshooting methodology provides a systematic approach to identifying and rectifying problems, minimizing downtime, and maintaining optimal network performance.

The first step in network troubleshooting is to gather information about the reported problem.

This involves talking to the user or stakeholder who reported the issue to understand the symptoms, such as network outages, slow performance, or connectivity problems.

Once you have a clear understanding of the problem, document it thoroughly, including the affected devices, applications, and the duration of the issue.

Having this information will help you narrow down potential causes and solutions.

The next step in the network troubleshooting methodology is to perform preliminary checks to rule out common issues.

This includes verifying physical connections, such as cables and power sources, to ensure that they are secure and functioning correctly.

Check the status of network devices, such as routers, switches, and access points, to see if they are powered on and operational.

Additionally, inspect the status indicators on these devices for any signs of trouble, such as flashing lights or error messages.

If you encounter any physical or hardware issues during this step, address them promptly to eliminate potential causes of the problem.

After performing preliminary checks, it's essential to isolate the issue and determine its scope.

This involves identifying whether the problem is affecting a single device, a specific subnet, or the entire network.

Use diagnostic tools and commands, such as ping or traceroute, to assess network connectivity between devices and subnets.

For instance, you can use the "ping" command to test the reachability of a specific device:

Copy code

```
ping 192.168.1.1
```

If the ping is successful, it indicates that the device is reachable over the network.

However, if the ping fails, it suggests a connectivity issue that needs further investigation.

To narrow down the scope of the problem, try pinging other devices or subnets to determine the extent of the issue.

Once you've isolated the problem to a specific device or network segment, focus your troubleshooting efforts in that area.

The next step involves analyzing network configurations and settings to identify potential misconfigurations or conflicts.

Check IP addresses, subnet masks, default gateways, and DNS settings to ensure that they are configured correctly on the affected device.

If you suspect a misconfiguration, correct it and test network connectivity again.

Network logs and error messages can provide valuable insights into the cause of the problem.

Review logs on network devices, servers, and applications to look for any errors or warnings that may indicate the root cause.

For example, you can use the "show log" command on a Cisco router to view the router's system logs:

bashCopy code

```
show log
```

Examine the logs for any entries related to the reported problem, and use the information to guide your troubleshooting efforts.

Sometimes, network issues may be related to software or firmware bugs.

Check for available updates or patches for network devices, operating systems, and applications to ensure that you are running the latest and most stable versions.

Apply necessary updates and test the network to see if the problem is resolved.

If you suspect that a device or application may be causing the issue, you can temporarily disconnect or disable it to see if network performance improves.

This can help isolate the problem and determine whether a particular device or application is the source of the trouble.

Network performance monitoring tools can provide valuable data on network utilization, bandwidth usage, and traffic patterns.

Use these tools to identify any abnormal network behavior or bottlenecks that may be causing the problem.

For example, you can use a tool like Wireshark to capture and analyze network traffic:

Copy code

```
wireshark
```

Wireshark allows you to examine packets in detail, helping you identify unusual or problematic traffic patterns.

After analyzing network configurations, logs, and traffic patterns, you may need to perform tests or experiments to further diagnose the issue.

For example, if you suspect that a network device is faulty, you can replace it with a known working device to see if the problem persists.

Similarly, if you suspect that a specific application is causing network congestion, you can temporarily disable it to observe the impact on network performance.

During the testing phase, document your findings and keep track of any changes or improvements in network behavior.

If the problem remains unresolved after conducting tests and experiments, consider seeking assistance from vendor support or consulting with colleagues who have expertise in network troubleshooting.

Vendor support can provide guidance, troubleshoot specific hardware or software issues, and help you implement solutions.

Collaborating with colleagues can bring fresh perspectives and insights that may lead to a breakthrough in resolving the problem.

When a solution is found, implement the necessary changes and verify that the issue is resolved.

Test the network thoroughly to ensure that all symptoms of the problem have been addressed.

Document the resolution, including the steps taken and any changes made to configurations or settings.

This documentation can be valuable for future reference and can help colleagues facing similar issues.

Finally, communicate the resolution to the user or stakeholder who reported the problem, and provide them with any necessary instructions or recommendations to prevent similar issues in the future.

In summary, a structured network troubleshooting methodology is essential for identifying and resolving network issues efficiently.

It involves gathering information, performing preliminary checks, isolating the problem, analyzing configurations, reviewing logs, testing, and seeking assistance when needed. By following a systematic approach, IT professionals can diagnose and resolve network problems effectively, ensuring that networks remain reliable and secure.

Network diagnostics are essential for identifying, analyzing, and resolving issues in computer networks, ensuring that they operate efficiently and deliver reliable connectivity to users.

Next, we will explore various tools and techniques that network professionals use to diagnose and troubleshoot network problems effectively.

One fundamental tool for network diagnostics is the command-line interface (CLI), which provides direct access to network devices and systems for monitoring and configuration.

Using the CLI, network administrators can execute commands and retrieve valuable information about the network's current state.

For example, the "ping" command is a widely used tool that sends ICMP echo requests to a target host to check its reachability and measure round-trip times:

Copy code

```
ping 192.168.1.1
```

The "ping" command can help determine if a network device is responsive or experiencing packet loss.

Another useful CLI tool is "traceroute" (or "tracert" on Windows), which traces the route packets take from the source to the destination, showing each hop along the way:

Copy code

```
traceroute www.example.com
```

This tool can help identify network delays or routing issues by displaying the IP addresses of intermediate routers and the time taken for packets to traverse each hop.

Network administrators often rely on packet capture and analysis tools like Wireshark to examine network traffic in detail.

Wireshark allows users to capture packets on a network interface, display packet contents, and filter traffic based on various criteria.

For example, to capture packets on interface eth0, you can use the following command:

cssCopy code

```
wireshark -i eth0
```

Wireshark can assist in diagnosing network issues by identifying abnormal or suspicious traffic patterns, such as excessive broadcast traffic or malformed packets.

Beyond capturing packets, Wireshark provides advanced features like protocol analysis and the ability to reconstruct and decode higher-layer protocols, making it a powerful tool for diagnosing complex network problems.

Network monitoring and management systems play a crucial role in network diagnostics, providing real-time visibility into network performance and device status.

Tools like Nagios, Zabbix, and PRTG Network Monitor can monitor network devices, services, and applications, generating alerts and reports based on predefined thresholds and conditions.

For example, Nagios can monitor the availability and response time of network services and notify administrators when issues are detected.

To deploy Nagios, administrators typically configure monitoring checks and define alerting criteria using its configuration files.

Security Information and Event Management (SIEM) systems, such as Splunk and ELK Stack, aggregate and correlate data from various sources, including network devices, to detect security threats and anomalies.

SIEM solutions use advanced analytics and machine learning algorithms to identify suspicious behavior and generate alerts for further investigation.

For example, a SIEM may detect multiple failed login attempts from a single IP address, indicating a potential brute-force attack.

Network professionals also employ network diagnostic utilities provided by operating systems, such as "netstat" and "ipconfig" on Windows, or "ifconfig" and "netstat" on Unix-based systems.

These utilities offer information about network interfaces, routing tables, active connections, and open ports.

For instance, the "netstat" command can display a list of active network connections on a Windows system:

Copy code

```
netstat -an
```

This output provides details about each connection, including the local and remote IP addresses, ports, and connection states.

In Unix-based systems, the "ifconfig" command displays network interface information, while "netstat" can reveal active network connections.

Effective network diagnostics also involve the use of specialized tools for specific tasks, such as network performance testing.

Tools like "iperf" allow network administrators to measure network bandwidth, latency, and throughput by generating traffic between two hosts:

csharpCopy code

iperf -s (on the server) iperf -c server_ip (on the client)

This command tests the network's performance between the server and client by sending data packets and measuring the transfer rate.

Wireless network diagnostics often require tools like "Wi-Fi analyzers" or "Wi-Fi scanners," which provide information about nearby Wi-Fi networks, signal strength, channel interference, and available access points.

Tools like "inSSIDer" or "NetSpot" on Windows and "Kismet" on Linux are commonly used for Wi-Fi diagnostics.

Network discovery and mapping tools, such as "nmap" or "Angry IP Scanner," can scan networks to identify active hosts, open ports, and services running on them.

For instance, the "nmap" command can perform a network scan of a target IP range:

Copy code

nmap -sP 192.168.1.0/24

This command identifies active hosts in the specified IP range.

Remote management and access tools like "SSH" and "Telnet" are indispensable for troubleshooting network devices remotely.

SSH (Secure Shell) provides encrypted remote access to network devices, allowing administrators to configure and diagnose issues securely.

To establish an SSH session, use a command like:

cssCopy code

ssh username @hostname

Telnet, although less secure, can be used to connect to devices that do not support SSH.

In addition to these tools, network professionals rely on documentation and network diagrams to aid in diagnostics.

Accurate network documentation, including IP address assignments, device configurations, and network topology, can expedite troubleshooting by providing clear insights into the network's architecture.

Network diagrams visually represent the network's structure, helping administrators visualize connections and device locations.

Using tools like Microsoft Visio or draw.io, network diagrams can be created and maintained to document changes and additions to the network.

To summarize, network diagnostics involve the use of a wide range of tools and techniques to identify, analyze, and resolve network issues.

These tools include command-line utilities, packet capture and analysis tools, network monitoring systems, SIEM solutions, network diagnostic utilities, specialized performance testing tools, wireless network analyzers, network discovery and mapping tools, and remote management and access tools.

Effective network diagnostics require a combination of these tools and techniques, along with documentation and network diagrams, to ensure the rapid and accurate resolution of network problems, minimizing downtime and maintaining network reliability.

*BOOK 2*
*NETWORK+ PROTOCOLS*
*INTERMEDIATE INSIGHTS*

*ROB BOTWRIGHT*

## Chapter 1: Review of Networking Fundamentals

Network models provide a structured framework for understanding and conceptualizing computer networks, offering a way to represent and analyze the complex interactions and components that make up these interconnected systems.

These models serve as valuable tools for network designers, administrators, and engineers to plan, implement, and troubleshoot networks effectively.

One of the earliest and most foundational network models is the OSI (Open Systems Interconnection) model, which was developed by the International Organization for Standardization (ISO) in the late 1970s.

The OSI model consists of seven distinct layers, each with a specific set of functions and responsibilities.

Starting from the lowest layer, Layer 1 (the Physical layer) deals with the physical transmission of data, including cables, switches, and electrical signals.

At Layer 2 (the Data Link layer), the model focuses on data framing, addressing, and error detection, often involving devices like switches and network interface cards (NICs).

Layer 3 (the Network layer) is responsible for routing packets between networks and utilizes routers to make forwarding decisions based on IP addresses.

Above that, Layer 4 (the Transport layer) manages end-to-end communication, providing flow control and error recovery through protocols like TCP (Transmission Control Protocol) and UDP (User Datagram Protocol).

Layer 5 (the Session layer) establishes, maintains, and terminates connections between applications, handling issues like session synchronization.

Layer 6 (the Presentation layer) deals with data translation and encryption, ensuring that data can be understood and interpreted correctly between systems.

Finally, Layer 7 (the Application layer) represents the topmost layer and includes the actual user-facing applications and services, such as web browsers and email clients.

The OSI model's advantage lies in its ability to divide the complex networking tasks into smaller, manageable layers, making it easier to design, troubleshoot, and understand network interactions.

A contrasting but widely used network model is the TCP/IP model, which consists of four layers: the Network Interface, Internet, Transport, and Application layers.

This model is more compact than the OSI model and is often favored for practical implementations because it closely mirrors the actual structure of the modern internet.

The Network Interface layer of the TCP/IP model corresponds to the Physical and Data Link layers of the OSI model, handling hardware-level details like MAC (Media Access Control) addresses and Ethernet frames.

Above that, the Internet layer is equivalent to the Network layer in the OSI model, responsible for routing packets between networks using IP addresses.

The Transport layer in the TCP/IP model maps to both the Transport and Session layers in the OSI model, managing end-to-end communication and providing error detection and recovery through protocols like TCP and UDP.

The topmost Application layer of the TCP/IP model covers Layers 5 through 7 of the OSI model, including the actual applications and services that users interact with, such as web browsers, email, and file transfer programs.

While the OSI model offers a more comprehensive and detailed breakdown of networking concepts, the TCP/IP model simplifies the layers, making it more practical for real-world networking scenarios.

In practice, both models serve as valuable reference points for understanding network protocols, components, and interactions.

Another important network model is the DoD (Department of Defense) model, which was developed in the 1970s by the U.S. Department of Defense as the foundation for the TCP/IP protocol suite.

The DoD model consists of four layers: the Process/Application layer, Host-to-Host layer, Internet layer, and Network Access layer.

Similar to the TCP/IP model, this model provides a conceptual framework for understanding network protocols and their functions.

The Process/Application layer in the DoD model aligns closely with the Application layer in the OSI model and encompasses user-facing applications and services.

The Host-to-Host layer corresponds to the Transport layer in the OSI model and manages end-to-end communication between hosts.

The Internet layer, like its counterpart in the TCP/IP model, focuses on routing packets between networks using IP addresses.

Finally, the Network Access layer encompasses the Physical and Data Link layers of the OSI model, handling hardware-level details and providing access to the physical network medium.

One of the key strengths of the DoD model is its direct association with the development of the TCP/IP protocol suite, making it a natural choice for understanding how these protocols fit together.

Each of these network models serves as a valuable tool for different purposes.

The OSI model provides a comprehensive framework for understanding network concepts and protocols in a structured manner, making it ideal for educational and theoretical contexts.

On the other hand, the TCP/IP model is often preferred for practical network design and troubleshooting due to its alignment with the architecture of the modern internet.

The DoD model bridges the gap between the theoretical and practical by connecting the TCP/IP protocol suite with a conceptual framework.

Ultimately, the choice of which network model to use depends on the specific context and requirements of network professionals and designers.

Understanding these models and their associated layers is crucial for anyone working in the field of networking, as they provide a common language and reference point for discussing network concepts and technologies.

By having a solid grasp of these models, network professionals can more effectively plan, design, implement, and troubleshoot complex networks, ensuring their reliability and performance.

Networking devices play a fundamental role in the creation and operation of computer networks, serving as the building blocks that enable the connectivity and communication of devices and users across a network.

These devices are essential components in the design and architecture of networks, and understanding their functions and capabilities is crucial for network professionals and administrators.

One of the most foundational networking devices is the network switch, which operates at the Data Link layer (Layer 2) of the OSI model.

A network switch connects devices within a local area network (LAN), using MAC addresses to forward data frames to their intended destinations.

Switches are essential for optimizing network performance by reducing collision domains and increasing the efficiency of data transmission within a LAN.

To manage a network switch, network administrators often use a CLI or a web-based interface to configure VLANs (Virtual LANs), set port configurations, and monitor network traffic.

For example, in a Cisco Catalyst switch, you can use the following CLI command to create a VLAN:

arduinoCopy code

switch(config)# vlan 10

This command creates a VLAN with the ID 10.

Another critical networking device is the router, which operates at the Network layer (Layer 3) of the OSI model.

Routers are responsible for forwarding data packets between different networks, using IP addresses to make routing decisions.

They serve as gateways that connect LANs to wide area networks (WANs) and the internet, enabling data to traverse diverse networks.

Configuring a router involves setting up routing protocols, defining access control lists (ACLs), and establishing NAT (Network Address Translation) rules.

For instance, to configure NAT on a Cisco router, you can use the following CLI commands:

scssCopy code

router(config)# access-list 1 permit 192.168.1.0 0.0.0.255

router(config)# ip nat inside source list 1 interface GigabitEthernet0/0 overload

These commands create an access list to specify which internal IP addresses should be translated and configure NAT overload on the router's interface.

Firewalls are another critical networking device, often situated at the perimeter of a network to enforce security policies and protect against unauthorized access and threats. Firewalls can operate at different layers of the OSI model, providing packet filtering, stateful inspection, and application-layer filtering.

Administrators configure firewall rules to control traffic flow based on criteria such as source IP, destination IP, port numbers, and application protocols.

For example, to create a firewall rule on a Cisco ASA firewall to allow HTTP traffic from a specific source IP address, you can use the following CLI commands:

scssCopy code

```
ciscoasa(config)# access-list outside_access_in extended permit tcp host 192.168.1.100 any eq http
ciscoasa(config)# access-group outside_access_in in interface outside
```

These commands create an access list permitting HTTP traffic from the source IP address 192.168.1.100 and apply it to the outside interface.

Access points (APs) are networking devices used to provide wireless connectivity within a LAN.

APs operate at the Data Link layer (Layer 2) and allow wireless devices such as laptops, smartphones, and tablets to connect to the network.

To configure a wireless access point, administrators typically use a web-based interface to set security settings, SSIDs (Service Set Identifiers), and wireless channels.

For example, to configure the security settings on a Cisco Aironet AP, you can use a web browser to access the AP's web-based management interface and navigate to the security settings section.

Hubs, though less commonly used today, are networking devices that operate at the Physical layer (Layer 1) and are responsible for connecting multiple devices within a LAN.

Unlike switches, hubs do not perform intelligent packet forwarding and instead broadcast data to all connected devices, creating a shared collision domain.

Network administrators rarely use hubs in modern networks due to their limited efficiency and security vulnerabilities.

Topology, in the context of computer networks, refers to the arrangement or layout of devices and connections within a network.

Network topologies can be classified into several types, including bus, star, ring, mesh, and hybrid topologies, each with its advantages and disadvantages.

A bus topology, for instance, consists of a single central cable to which all devices are connected, while a star topology features a central hub or switch with individual connections to each device.

A ring topology connects devices in a closed loop, where data circulates in one direction, while a mesh topology involves interconnecting devices with multiple redundant paths for fault tolerance.

Hybrid topologies combine elements of different topologies to meet specific network requirements.

To create a network topology, administrators use network design tools or software to plan and visualize the arrangement of devices, cables, and connections.

These tools help ensure that the network meets performance, redundancy, and scalability requirements.

For example, to design a network topology, administrators can use software like Cisco Packet Tracer or GNS3 to simulate and visualize the network layout, test configurations, and assess the network's behavior.

When deploying a network, administrators must consider factors such as scalability, reliability, and ease of management.

The choice of networking devices and topology depends on the organization's specific needs, budget constraints, and performance requirements.

For example, a small office network may opt for a simple star topology with a single switch, while a large enterprise might implement a complex mesh topology with redundant links for high availability.

Additionally, network professionals must consider factors like security, data traffic patterns, and the growth potential of the network when designing and deploying networking solutions.

In summary, networking devices and topologies form the foundation of computer networks, enabling the connectivity and communication of devices and users.

Network switches, routers, firewalls, access points, and hubs each serve distinct roles in network architecture.

Understanding their functions and configurations is crucial for network professionals to design, implement, and manage networks effectively.

## Chapter 2: Advanced IP Addressing and Subnetting

Variable Length Subnet Masking (VLSM) is a network addressing technique that allows network administrators to allocate subnets with different sizes (subnets with variable lengths) within a larger network address space.

VLSM is a powerful and flexible approach to subnetting that maximizes IP address utilization, reduces waste, and enhances network efficiency.

Traditional subnetting, also known as fixed-length subnet masking (FLSM), divides a network into equal-sized subnets, where each subnet has the same number of host addresses.

For example, if you have a Class C network with a default subnet mask of 255.255.255.0, you would typically create eight subnets, each accommodating 254 hosts.

In FLSM, this approach works well when all subnets require the same number of hosts, but it often leads to inefficient IP address allocation.

VLSM, on the other hand, allows network administrators to allocate subnets based on the specific needs of each network segment.

This means that subnets can have varying sizes, with some subnets having more host addresses than others.

To implement VLSM, you need to plan your subnetting carefully, starting with the largest subnets and gradually moving to smaller ones.

Let's illustrate VLSM with an example:

Suppose you have a Class C network with the address 192.168.1.0 and a default subnet mask of 255.255.255.0.

You want to allocate subnets for three departments: Sales, Marketing, and IT.

Sales requires the largest subnet with 60 hosts, Marketing needs a subnet with 30 hosts, and IT needs a subnet with 10 hosts.

In a VLSM scenario, you would start by creating the largest subnet for Sales.

To accommodate 60 hosts, you need a subnet with at least 64 ($2^6$) addresses. Therefore, you would use a subnet mask of 255.255.255.192 (/26).

The subnet for Sales would be:

Network Address: 192.168.1.0/26

Usable IP Range: 192.168.1.1 to 192.168.1.62

Broadcast Address: 192.168.1.63

Now, you have allocated the largest subnet to Sales while conserving IP addresses efficiently.

Next, you move on to Marketing, which requires a subnet for 30 hosts.

To accommodate 30 hosts, you need a subnet with at least 32 ($2^5$) addresses. Therefore, you would use a subnet mask of 255.255.255.224 (/27).

The subnet for Marketing would be:

Network Address: 192.168.1.64/27

Usable IP Range: 192.168.1.65 to 192.168.1.94

Broadcast Address: 192.168.1.95

Now, you have allocated a subnet for Marketing while efficiently using IP addresses.

Finally, you address the IT department, which requires a subnet for 10 hosts.

To accommodate 10 hosts, you need a subnet with at least 16 ($2^4$) addresses. Therefore, you would use a subnet mask of 255.255.255.240 (/28).

The subnet for IT would be:

Network Address: 192.168.1.96/28

Usable IP Range: 192.168.1.97 to 192.168.1.110

Broadcast Address: 192.168.1.111

By using VLSM, you have efficiently allocated subnets to each department based on their specific requirements.

This approach minimizes IP address wastage, as each subnet has just enough addresses to meet its needs.

To configure VLSM on network devices, such as routers, you would create subinterfaces on router interfaces and assign the appropriate subnet masks to each subinterface.

For example, on a Cisco router, you can create subinterfaces on a physical interface and assign IP addresses and subnet masks using the following CLI commands:

kotlinCopy code

interface GigabitEthernet0/0.10 encapsulation dot1Q 10 ip address 192.168.1.1 255.255.255.192 ! interface GigabitEthernet0/0.20 encapsulation dot1Q 20 ip address 192.168.1.65 255.255.255.224 ! interface GigabitEthernet0/0.30 encapsulation dot1Q 30 ip address 192.168.1.97 255.255.255.240

These commands configure subinterfaces for VLANs 10, 20, and 30, each with its specific subnet and mask.

In VLSM, careful planning is essential to ensure that subnets do not overlap or conflict with each other.

Additionally, you must document the allocation of subnets and their associated masks to maintain a clear record of the network's addressing scheme.

VLSM is a powerful tool for network administrators, enabling efficient IP address allocation in networks with varying subnet size requirements.

By tailoring subnets to match the specific needs of each network segment, VLSM reduces IP address waste and maximizes network efficiency, contributing to effective IP address management in modern networks.

CIDR notation, which stands for Classless Inter-Domain

Routing notation, is a compact and flexible way to represent IP addresses and their associated subnet masks.

It is widely used in network configuration, routing tables, and communication between network professionals to simplify and standardize IP address notation.

CIDR notation consists of an IP address followed by a forward slash ("/") and a numerical value representing the prefix length.

The prefix length indicates the number of bits in the subnet mask that are set to 1.

For example, the CIDR notation "192.168.1.0/24" represents an IP address of 192.168.1.0 with a subnet mask of 255.255.255.0.

In this notation, the "/24" signifies that the first 24 bits of the subnet mask are set to 1, leaving the last 8 bits for host addresses.

CIDR notation provides a way to express network addresses with variable-length subnet masks, allowing for efficient IP address allocation and route summarization.

To understand CIDR notation further, let's explore some common prefix lengths and their meanings:

"/32" represents a host address with no subnet bits, meaning it is an individual IP address. For example, "192.168.1.1/32" represents the specific host 192.168.1.1.

"/24" represents a typical Class C network with a subnet mask of 255.255.255.0. It allows for up to 254 host addresses within the network.

"/16" represents a Class B network with a subnet mask of 255.255.0.0. It allows for up to 65,534 host addresses within the network.

"/8" represents a Class A network with a subnet mask of 255.0.0.0. It allows for up to 16,777,214 host addresses within the network.

CIDR notation can also express more specific subnets by using higher prefix lengths.

For example, "/28" represents a subnet with 16 host addresses, while "/30" represents a subnet with only 2 host addresses.

CIDR notation is particularly useful when working with routing protocols, such as BGP (Border Gateway Protocol), where route summarization and efficient use of IP address space are essential.

When configuring routing on network devices, you can use CIDR notation to define route prefixes and specify which networks can be reached through a particular interface.

For example, on a Cisco router, you can configure a static route using CIDR notation like this:

Copy code

**ip route 192.168.10.0 255.255.255.0 192.168.1.2**

In this command, "192.168.10.0/24" represents the destination network, "255.255.255.0" is the subnet mask, and "192.168.1.2" is the next-hop router's IP address.

CIDR notation simplifies route configuration by providing a concise way to represent network prefixes and their masks.

CIDR notation also plays a significant role in IP address allocation and management, allowing organizations to efficiently allocate address space while minimizing waste.

For example, an organization may receive a block of IP addresses from a regional internet registry (RIR) and use CIDR notation to allocate subnets of various sizes to different departments or locations within the organization.

This approach ensures that IP address space is used optimally and that smaller subnets are allocated where needed, reducing IP address waste.

CIDR notation can also help network administrators plan and document their network addressing schemes effectively.

By using CIDR notation, administrators can clearly express the size and purpose of each subnet, making it easier to manage and troubleshoot the network.

Additionally, CIDR notation is a crucial concept for network certification exams, as it is a fundamental skill for network professionals.

For example, in Cisco's CCNA (Cisco Certified Network Associate) exam, candidates are expected to understand CIDR notation and its role in subnetting, routing, and IP address management.

In summary, CIDR notation is a concise and flexible way to represent IP addresses and subnet masks, allowing for efficient IP address allocation, route summarization, and network documentation.

It simplifies route configuration in network devices, enhances IP address management, and is a fundamental skill for network professionals.

## Chapter 3: Dynamic Routing Protocols

The Open Shortest Path First (OSPF) routing protocol is a widely used interior gateway protocol (IGP) that plays a critical role in routing and maintaining the connectivity of IP networks.

OSPF is known for its efficiency, scalability, and support for complex network topologies, making it a fundamental topic in the field of networking.

Originally developed as an open standard by the Internet Engineering Task Force (IETF), OSPF is designed to efficiently determine the best path for data packets to traverse a network.

One of the key principles of OSPF is its link-state routing algorithm, which is based on the idea that each router maintains a database of information about the state of its directly connected links.

This database, known as the Link-State Database (LSDB), contains information about the network topology, including the status and cost of each link.

OSPF routers use this LSDB to calculate the shortest path tree (also known as the SPF tree) to all reachable destinations in the network.

The result of this calculation is the routing table, which specifies the best path to reach each destination based on the SPF tree.

OSPF routers exchange routing information using OSPF packets, which are encapsulated within IP packets.

These OSPF packets are used to share information about link states, perform neighbor discovery, and synchronize LSDBs among routers.

OSPF routers in the same OSPF area maintain synchronized LSDBs, ensuring that they have a consistent view of the network topology.

OSPF uses a hierarchical network design with multiple areas, and routers within the same area share LSDBs.

This hierarchical structure improves scalability and reduces the amount of routing information that needs to be exchanged across the entire network.

OSPF areas are organized in a hierarchical manner, with a backbone area (Area 0) serving as the central core of the OSPF network.

Routers in different areas can summarize their routing information when advertising routes to routers in other areas, further enhancing scalability.

One of the advantages of OSPF is its ability to support variable-length subnet masks (VLSM) and classless inter-domain routing (CIDR), allowing for efficient use of IP address space.

OSPF can also carry routing information for multiple IP address families, including IPv4 and IPv6, making it versatile for modern network environments.

When configuring OSPF on network devices, such as routers, network administrators use the command-line interface (CLI) to define OSPF areas, enable OSPF routing on interfaces, and specify OSPF router IDs.

For instance, on a Cisco router, you can configure OSPF in the following way:

arduinoCopy code

router(config)# router ospf 1 router(config-router)# network 192.168.1.0 0.0.0.255 area 0

In this example, "router ospf 1" enters OSPF configuration mode, and "network 192.168.1.0 0.0.0.255 area 0" specifies the network to be advertised into OSPF and the associated OSPF area.

OSPF also supports authentication mechanisms to secure routing updates exchanged between routers.

For example, you can configure OSPF authentication using the following CLI commands:

arduinoCopy code

```
router(config)# interface GigabitEthernet0/0 router(config-if)# ip ospf authentication message-digest router(config-if)# ip ospf message-digest-key 1 md5 MySecretKey
```

These commands enable OSPF message digest authentication and define a shared secret key.

OSPF routers in the same area must use the same authentication settings to establish neighbor relationships and exchange routing information.

One of the unique features of OSPF is its support for equal-cost multipath (ECMP) routing.

When OSPF calculates the SPF tree and identifies multiple equal-cost paths to a destination, it can install all of these paths in the routing table.

This allows OSPF to load balance traffic across multiple links, improving network utilization and fault tolerance.

To view the OSPF routing table on a Cisco router, you can use the "show ip route" command, which displays the list of OSPF-learned routes, their next-hop routers, and associated metrics.

OSPF also provides mechanisms for route summarization, allowing routers to advertise summarized routes instead of individual subnets.

This reduces the size of OSPF routing updates and improves network convergence.

Summarization is particularly useful when dealing with large IP address spaces or complex network designs.

In summary, OSPF is a robust and efficient routing protocol that plays a crucial role in the functioning of IP networks.

Its link-state routing algorithm, hierarchical design, support for variable-length subnet masks, and authentication mechanisms make it a versatile choice for network administrators.

By configuring OSPF on network devices and understanding its principles, network professionals can ensure optimal routing and connectivity in their networks, whether they are small LANs or large-scale enterprise environments.

The Enhanced Interior Gateway Routing Protocol (EIGRP) is a dynamic routing protocol that plays a crucial role in determining optimal paths for data packets within an IP network.

EIGRP is proprietary to Cisco Systems but has been widely adopted in Cisco-centric network environments.

It is classified as a hybrid routing protocol, combining features of both distance-vector and link-state routing protocols, which gives it unique advantages in terms of speed, efficiency, and convergence.

EIGRP uses a metric called the "composite metric" to calculate the best path to a destination network.

This metric takes into account multiple factors, including bandwidth, delay, reliability, and load, allowing EIGRP to make intelligent routing decisions.

EIGRP routers maintain a routing table that contains information about known networks, along with the associated metrics.

To configure EIGRP on a Cisco router, network administrators use the command-line interface (CLI) to enter EIGRP configuration mode and specify relevant parameters.

For example, to enable EIGRP routing on a router and specify an autonomous system number (ASN), you can use the following CLI commands:

arduinoCopy code

router (config) # router eigrp 100

In this command, "router eigrp 100" enables EIGRP with an ASN of 100.

EIGRP uses autonomous system numbers (ASNs) to identify separate EIGRP routing domains within an IP network.

Within an EIGRP routing domain, routers exchange routing information to build and maintain their routing tables.

EIGRP routers discover their neighbors using a mechanism known as the "Hello protocol."

When routers share Hello packets on directly connected interfaces, they establish neighbor relationships and exchange routing information.

EIGRP routers also exchange updates called "EIGRP Update" packets, which contain information about network routes and their associated metrics.

These updates help routers build a topological map of the network, allowing them to calculate the best paths efficiently.

EIGRP supports classless routing, meaning it can route IP networks with variable-length subnet masks (VLSM) and classless inter-domain routing (CIDR).

This flexibility allows network administrators to make efficient use of IP address space by creating subnets of varying sizes.

EIGRP can also provide route summarization, reducing the size of routing tables by advertising summarized routes instead of individual subnets.

This feature is particularly beneficial in large network environments.

EIGRP supports route redistribution, enabling routers to exchange routing information with routers running different routing protocols.

For example, a router running EIGRP can redistribute routes learned from OSPF or RIP into the EIGRP domain, allowing for seamless routing between different parts of the network.

To configure route redistribution in EIGRP, network administrators use the "redistribute" command in EIGRP configuration mode.

EIGRP also incorporates features for load balancing and equal-cost multipath (ECMP) routing.

When multiple routes to a destination network have equal metrics, EIGRP can install all of these routes in the routing table, distributing traffic across multiple paths.

This load-balancing capability enhances network performance and fault tolerance.

EIGRP routers use a proprietary protocol known as the Reliable Transport Protocol (RTP) for exchanging routing updates.

RTP ensures the reliable delivery of EIGRP packets, minimizing the risk of routing loops or data loss.

EIGRP is known for its rapid convergence time, which is the speed at which routers adapt to changes in the network topology.

When a network link or router fails, EIGRP routers quickly update their routing tables and recompute routes, minimizing disruption to network traffic.

Administrators can also fine-tune EIGRP convergence behavior using various timers and parameters.

For instance, the "hello-interval" and "hold-time" timers can be adjusted to control how often routers send Hello packets and when they consider a neighbor to have failed.

In summary, the Enhanced Interior Gateway Routing Protocol (EIGRP) is a powerful routing protocol that provides efficient and rapid routing in IP networks.

Its hybrid nature, support for VLSM and CIDR, route summarization, route redistribution, load balancing, and fast convergence make it a versatile choice for network administrators.

By configuring EIGRP on network devices and understanding its principles, network professionals can ensure optimal routing and performance in their Cisco-based networks, from small LANs to complex enterprise environments.

## Chapter 4: Switching and Virtual LANs (VLANs)

Virtual LANs (VLANs) are a fundamental networking technology that allows network administrators to segment a physical network into multiple logical networks, providing isolation, security, and efficient traffic management.

VLANs are an essential part of modern network design, offering flexibility and scalability in various network environments.

When configuring VLANs on network devices, such as switches, network administrators use the command-line interface (CLI) to create and manage VLANs.

For example, on a Cisco switch, you can create a VLAN using the following CLI command:

arduinoCopy code

Switch (config) # vlan 10

In this command, "vlan 10" creates a VLAN with the identifier 10.

VLANs are typically assigned unique identifiers known as VLAN IDs, ranging from 1 to 4095, depending on the networking equipment and standards used.

Each VLAN represents a separate broadcast domain, meaning devices within the same VLAN can communicate with each other as if they were on the same physical network, while devices in different VLANs are isolated by default.

This isolation provides several benefits, such as improved network security and broadcast domain segmentation.

One common use case for VLANs is separating user devices (e.g., PCs, laptops) from network infrastructure devices (e.g., servers, routers) to enhance security.

VLANs also enable network administrators to group devices logically based on their functions or departments, facilitating easier management and troubleshooting.

To assign a VLAN to a switch interface, administrators use the "switchport access vlan" CLI command.

For example, to assign VLAN 10 to an interface, you can use the following command:

arduinoCopy code

Switch (config-if)# switchport mode access Switch (config-if)# switchport access vlan 10

In this example, "switchport mode access" sets the interface as an access port, and "switchport access vlan 10" assigns VLAN 10 to the interface.

Access ports belong to a single VLAN and carry traffic only for that VLAN.

Another important concept in VLAN configuration is trunking, which allows multiple VLANs to traverse a single physical link between network devices, typically switches.

Trunking is essential for interconnecting switches and routers while preserving the segregation of VLANs.

On Cisco switches, the "switchport mode trunk" CLI command configures an interface as a trunk port.

For example:

arduinoCopy code

Switch (config-if)# switchport mode trunk

Trunk ports can carry traffic for multiple VLANs simultaneously by adding a VLAN tag (also known as a VLAN ID or VLAN header) to each Ethernet frame.

This tagging allows switches to differentiate traffic from different VLANs when it traverses the trunk link.

Common trunking protocols include IEEE 802.1Q and Cisco's proprietary Inter-Switch Link (ISL).

To configure trunking with 802.1Q on a Cisco switch interface, you can use the following CLI command:

arduinoCopy code

Switch (config-if)# switchport trunk encapsulation dot1q

This command configures the interface to use 802.1Q encapsulation for trunking.

After configuring trunking, network administrators can specify which VLANs should be allowed to traverse the trunk link using the "switchport trunk allowed vlan" command.

For example:

arduinoCopy code

Switch (config-if)# switchport trunk allowed vlan 10,20,30

In this command, VLANs 10, 20, and 30 are allowed to pass through the trunk link.

Trunk ports also support a feature called native VLAN, which is the VLAN that carries untagged traffic across the trunk link.

By default, VLAN 1 is the native VLAN on Cisco switches, but administrators can change it as needed.

To set the native VLAN on a trunk port, you can use the "switchport trunk native vlan" command:

arduinoCopy code

Switch (config-if)# switchport trunk native vlan 99

In this example, VLAN 99 is configured as the native VLAN.

It's important to ensure that the native VLAN on both ends of a trunk link matches to avoid connectivity issues.

VLANs and trunking are integral to the operation of Virtual LANs, enabling network administrators to create flexible, segmented networks that support various network services and security requirements.

VLANs can also be used in conjunction with other networking technologies, such as Virtual Routing and

Forwarding (VRF) and Quality of Service (QoS), to enhance network functionality and performance.

Additionally, VLANs play a crucial role in cloud environments and data center networks, where virtualization and network isolation are essential for efficient resource management and security.

Overall, understanding VLAN configuration and trunking is essential for network professionals responsible for designing and maintaining complex and efficient network infrastructures.

VLAN troubleshooting is a critical skill for network administrators because VLANs are an integral part of modern network design, providing segmentation and isolation of network traffic for enhanced security and performance.

When network issues arise within VLANs, it's essential to diagnose and resolve them promptly to ensure the smooth operation of the network.

One common VLAN troubleshooting technique is to verify VLAN configuration settings on network devices, such as switches and routers.

Using the command-line interface (CLI) or graphical user interface (GUI) of these devices, administrators can review VLAN assignments, port configurations, and trunking settings.

For example, to check VLAN configurations on a Cisco switch, you can use the "show vlan" command:

arduinoCopy code

```
Switch# show vlan
```

This command displays a list of configured VLANs, their VLAN IDs, and associated ports.

Inspecting the output can help identify any misconfigurations or inconsistencies in VLAN assignments.

Another aspect to investigate is the status of VLAN interfaces on Layer 3 devices like routers.

The "show ip interface brief" command on a Cisco router provides information about the operational status of VLAN interfaces:

kotlinCopy code

Router# show ip interface brief

By examining this output, administrators can determine if VLAN interfaces are up and if the correct IP addresses are assigned to them.

Additionally, network administrators should inspect the status of trunk links between switches and routers, as misconfigured trunk ports can lead to VLAN communication issues.

To view trunk port status on a Cisco switch, you can use the "show interfaces trunk" command:

arduinoCopy code

Switch# show interfaces trunk

This command displays trunk port information, including VLANs allowed and encapsulation methods.

Errors or inconsistencies in trunk settings can be detected and resolved by reviewing this output.

Another important VLAN troubleshooting technique involves checking for network connectivity issues within VLANs.

Network administrators can use tools like the "ping" command to test connectivity between devices within the same VLAN.

For instance, to test connectivity between two devices in VLAN 10, you can use the following CLI command:

arduinoCopy code

DeviceA# ping DeviceB

A successful ping indicates that devices in the same VLAN can communicate with each other.

If the ping fails, administrators should examine the following:

Verify that both devices are in the same VLAN by checking their port configurations on the switch.

Ensure that the devices have the correct IP addresses and subnet masks within the same subnet.

Confirm that there are no firewall rules or access control lists (ACLs) blocking traffic within the VLAN.

Inter-VLAN routing issues can also cause communication problems between VLANs.

Network administrators should check the configuration of the router responsible for routing traffic between VLANs.

Using the CLI, they can examine routing tables, access lists, and router interfaces.

For example, to view the routing table on a Cisco router, you can use the "show ip route" command:

arduinoCopy code

```
Router# show ip route
```

This command displays the router's routing table, including routes to different VLANs.

If the routing table does not contain entries for the VLANs or if there are routing protocol issues, this can lead to inter-VLAN communication problems.

Network administrators should also consider the possibility of VLAN tagging issues on trunk links.

VLAN tags are essential for distinguishing traffic from different VLANs on trunked links.

Using the "show interfaces" command on a Cisco switch, administrators can inspect the statistics for incoming and outgoing traffic on trunk interfaces:

arduinoCopy code

```
Switch# show interfaces gigabitethernet0/1
```

If a trunk link is dropping or discarding frames from specific VLANs, it may indicate VLAN tagging problems or issues with native VLAN settings.

Monitoring the trunk interface's statistics can help identify anomalies. VLANs can also experience issues related to broadcast storms or excessive multicast traffic.

These issues can lead to network congestion and performance problems. Administrators can use network monitoring tools to analyze network traffic and identify the source of excessive broadcast or multicast traffic.

Once identified, they can implement strategies to mitigate the issue, such as implementing broadcast storm control or optimizing multicast traffic.

It's also important to consider VLAN security concerns during troubleshooting. Ensure that the appropriate security measures, such as access control lists (ACLs) and VLAN-based firewall rules, are in place to prevent unauthorized access or traffic between VLANs. By regularly reviewing and adjusting these security measures, network administrators can minimize security risks within VLANs.

In summary, VLAN troubleshooting techniques are essential for maintaining the stability and reliability of network environments that rely on VLAN segmentation.

Network administrators should be proficient in verifying VLAN configurations, checking connectivity, inspecting inter-VLAN routing, investigating trunking issues, monitoring traffic, and addressing security concerns to effectively diagnose and resolve VLAN-related problems.

By mastering these techniques, network professionals can ensure that VLANs continue to provide the desired level of network isolation and performance in various network architectures and scenarios.

## Chapter 5: Network Address Translation (NAT) and Port Forwarding

Network Address Translation (NAT) is a critical networking technology that allows multiple devices on a local network to share a single public IP address when communicating with external networks, such as the internet.

NAT plays a crucial role in conserving IPv4 address space and enabling private networks to access resources on the global internet.

There are different types of NAT, each serving specific purposes and providing varying degrees of functionality and security.

Static NAT, also known as one-to-one NAT, is a type of NAT that maps a specific private IP address to a corresponding public IP address.

This mapping remains constant, allowing external devices to initiate connections to the internal device using its public IP address.

To configure static NAT on a Cisco router, you can use the following CLI command:

scssCopy code

Router(config)# ip nat inside source static [private IP] [public IP]

This command establishes a static NAT mapping between the private IP and the public IP.

Static NAT is often used for scenarios where an internal server, such as a web server or mail server, needs to be accessible from the internet using a consistent public IP address.

Dynamic NAT, on the other hand, is a type of NAT that assigns a public IP address from a pool of available addresses to internal devices on a first-come, first-served basis.

The mapping between private and public IP addresses is temporary and can change as devices establish and release connections.

To configure dynamic NAT on a Cisco router, you can use the following CLI commands:

scssCopy code

Router(config)# ip nat pool [pool name] [start public IP] [end public IP] netmask [subnet mask] Router(config)# access-list [ACL number] permit [source network] Router(config)# ip nat inside source list [ACL number] pool [pool name]

These commands define a pool of public IP addresses, create an access control list (ACL) to specify the source network eligible for NAT, and configure dynamic NAT using the ACL and the pool.

Dynamic NAT is commonly used when a limited number of public IP addresses are available, and devices on the internal network need internet access without exposing their private IP addresses directly.

Port Address Translation (PAT), also known as Network Address Port Translation (NAPT), is a variation of NAT that maps multiple private IP addresses to a single public IP address using different source port numbers.

PAT is commonly used in home and small office routers to allow multiple devices to share a single public IP address.

When configuring PAT on a Cisco router, you can use the following CLI command:

scssCopy code

Router(config)# ip nat inside source list [ACL number] interface [interface] overload

110

This command specifies an ACL that identifies the internal devices eligible for NAT and assigns them a dynamic port on the router's interface.

PAT is effective in conserving public IP addresses and is often used in scenarios where a large number of devices need internet access.

NAT also plays a significant role in the deployment of IPv6 in networks that primarily use IPv4.

IPv6 transition mechanisms, such as Network Address Translation IPv6 to IPv4 (NAT64), allow devices on IPv6 networks to access IPv4 resources on the internet by performing translation between IPv6 and IPv4 addresses.

Configuring NAT64 on a router involves mapping IPv6 addresses to corresponding IPv4 addresses and defining translation rules.

NAT64 is vital in facilitating the coexistence of IPv6 and IPv4 in today's mixed networking environments.

In addition to NAT types, NAT configuration also involves defining translation rules and access control to control which devices are subject to NAT and which traffic is allowed or denied.

Access control lists (ACLs) are a fundamental component of NAT configuration, specifying the criteria for selecting traffic to be translated.

For example, to create an ACL to match a range of internal IP addresses, you can use the following CLI command:

scssCopy code

Router(config)# access-list [ACL number] permit ip [source network] [source wildcard] [destination network] [destination wildcard]

This command defines an ACL that permits traffic from a specific source network to a specific destination network.

ACLs are then referenced in NAT configuration commands to determine which traffic should undergo NAT.

It is crucial to craft ACLs carefully to ensure that the intended traffic is translated, while undesired traffic is not.

Furthermore, NAT can introduce certain challenges, such as the potential for translation table exhaustion or the need for hairpinning (local traffic returning through the NAT device).

To address these challenges, administrators should monitor NAT translation tables, adjust timeouts as needed, and implement hairpinning rules when necessary.

NAT configuration is a fundamental aspect of network design and security, as it determines how devices on a local network interact with external networks and services.

Understanding the various NAT types, their use cases, and the configuration of translation rules and ACLs is essential for network administrators to ensure proper connectivity, security, and resource conservation in their networks.

NAT plays a critical role in enabling multiple devices to share limited public IP addresses, a practice that has become increasingly important with the depletion of IPv4 addresses and the adoption of IPv6 transition mechanisms.

Port forwarding and Port Address Translation (PAT) are essential networking techniques that enable devices on a local network to provide services or applications accessible from the internet while using a single public IP address.

These techniques are widely used in home networks, small offices, and enterprise environments to facilitate remote access and host various services.

Port forwarding involves redirecting incoming network traffic from a specific port on a router or firewall to a designated device on the local network.

This technique is particularly useful when hosting services such as web servers, online gaming servers, or remote desktop services.

To configure port forwarding on a router, network administrators typically access the router's web-based interface and navigate to the port forwarding or virtual server section.

Within this section, administrators specify the external port (the port on the public IP address) and the internal IP address of the device providing the service, along with the internal port (the port on the local device).

For example, to configure port forwarding for a web server, the following settings may be used:

External Port: 80 (HTTP)

Internal IP Address: 192.168.1.100 (the IP address of the web server)

Internal Port: 80 (the default HTTP port)

This configuration instructs the router to forward incoming HTTP traffic (on port 80) to the local web server.

As a result, users from the internet can access the web server's content using the router's public IP address.

Port forwarding is versatile and can be used to host various services on different devices within a network, provided that each service uses a unique port number.

Port Address Translation (PAT), also known as Network Address Port Translation (NAPT), is a variant of Network Address Translation (NAT) that allows multiple devices on a local network to share a single public IP address.

PAT uses unique port numbers to differentiate between internal devices, enabling multiple devices to use the same public IP address simultaneously.

This technique is commonly used in home and small office routers to enable multiple devices to access the internet using a single public IP address.

To configure PAT on a router, network administrators specify the external port range to be used for translation.

For example, a router may be configured to use port numbers from 50000 to 60000 for PAT.

When devices on the local network initiate outbound connections to the internet, the router assigns each connection a unique port number within the specified range. This unique combination of source IP address, source port, destination IP address, and destination port allows the router to keep track of the connections and properly route responses back to the correct internal device.

Port forwarding and PAT are crucial for allowing remote access to services hosted within a private network.

For example, configuring port forwarding for Remote Desktop Protocol (RDP) on a router allows users to connect to a specific computer within the local network from a remote location.

Similarly, PAT enables multiple devices within a home or office network to browse the web or access online services using a single public IP address.

It's important to note that while these techniques provide convenience and functionality, they also introduce security considerations.

Opening specific ports through port forwarding can expose services to potential threats from the internet, making it essential to implement proper security measures, such as access control lists (ACLs) and firewall rules, to restrict access to authorized sources.

Additionally, routers often provide the option to change the default ports for certain services to enhance security further.

When configuring port forwarding or PAT, administrators should consider the security implications and implement best practices to safeguard the local network.

In summary, port forwarding and PAT are vital networking techniques that enable devices within a private network to provide services or access the internet using a single public IP address.

These techniques offer flexibility and convenience for hosting services and facilitating remote access.

However, administrators should prioritize security by implementing proper access controls, monitoring traffic, and considering port changes for enhanced protection against potential threats.

## Chapter 6: Quality of Service (QoS) and Traffic Shaping

Quality of Service (QoS) mechanisms and prioritization techniques are fundamental aspects of network management that ensure the efficient delivery of data and applications while meeting performance and service-level objectives.

QoS is crucial in today's networks, where various types of traffic, including voice, video, and data, compete for bandwidth.

One of the primary goals of QoS is to prioritize critical traffic to ensure low latency, minimal packet loss, and high overall network performance.

To deploy QoS effectively, network administrators need to understand the mechanisms involved and implement prioritization techniques tailored to their network's specific requirements.

A key QoS mechanism is traffic classification, which involves categorizing network traffic into different classes or service levels based on specific attributes, such as the type of application, source, or destination.

For example, Voice over IP (VoIP) traffic may be classified as a high-priority class, while bulk file transfers are placed in a lower-priority class.

Network administrators can use classification techniques, such as Deep Packet Inspection (DPI) or the Differentiated Services Code Point (DSCP) field in IP headers, to identify and classify traffic.

Once traffic is classified, QoS policies can be applied to prioritize and shape the flow of packets within the network.

One common QoS technique is Traffic Policing, which enforces traffic rate limits for specific classes of traffic.

Administrators can configure Traffic Policing using CLI commands on network devices like routers or switches.

For instance, on a Cisco router, the following command may be used to apply Traffic Policing to a specific class of traffic: scssCopy code

Router(config)# class-map [class name] Router(config-cmap)# match [criteria] Router(config)# policy-map [policy name] Router(config-pmap)# class [class name] Router(config-pmap-c)# police [rate] [burst size]

This configuration specifies the class of traffic to police, sets the rate limit, and defines the burst size for the traffic class.

Traffic exceeding the specified rate limit may be dropped or marked for a lower priority class, preventing it from congesting the network.

Another QoS mechanism is Traffic Shaping, which shapes traffic by buffering packets and smoothing their transmission rate.

Traffic Shaping is particularly useful for preventing bursty traffic from overwhelming network links and causing congestion.

Administrators can configure Traffic Shaping using CLI commands on network devices.

For example, on a Cisco router, the following command may be used to shape traffic: scssCopy code

Router(config)# policy-map [policy name] Router(config-pmap)# class [class name] Router(config-pmap-c)# shape [average rate] [burst size]

This configuration defines a policy map, specifies the class of traffic to shape, and sets the desired average rate and burst size for the traffic class.

Traffic shaping helps ensure that traffic conforms to the specified rate limits, preventing network congestion and maintaining consistent performance.

Queuing and scheduling are critical QoS mechanisms for controlling the order in which packets are transmitted from network queues.

Different queuing algorithms prioritize packets based on specific criteria, such as priority, class, or type of traffic.

Administrators can configure queuing mechanisms using CLI commands on network devices.

For example, on a Cisco router, the following command may be used to configure a priority queue for VoIP traffic:

scssCopy code

Router(config)# policy-map [policy name] Router(config-pmap)# class [class name] Router(config-pmap-c)# priority [bandwidth]

This configuration creates a policy map, assigns a traffic class, and allocates a specific amount of bandwidth to the priority queue, ensuring that VoIP traffic receives preferential treatment.

Weighted Fair Queuing (WFQ) is another queuing algorithm that assigns weights to different traffic classes, allowing higher-priority classes to receive a larger share of bandwidth during congestion.

Administrators can configure WFQ using CLI commands on network devices.

For instance, on a Cisco router, the following command may be used to configure WFQ:

scssCopy code

Router(config)# class-map [class name] Router(config-cmap)# match [criteria] Router(config)# policy-map [policy name] Router(config-pmap)# class [class name] Router(config-pmap-c)# fair-queue [bandwidth]

This configuration defines a class map, matches specific criteria, creates a policy map, assigns a traffic class, and allocates bandwidth using fair queuing.

Beyond queuing, network administrators may implement Explicit Congestion Notification (ECN) and Random Early Detection (RED) mechanisms to proactively manage congestion and prevent packet drops.

ECN marks packets to indicate network congestion, allowing routers and switches to signal congestion to endpoints, which can then adjust their transmission rates.

RED, on the other hand, randomly drops packets before network congestion reaches critical levels, encouraging congestion-aware behavior from endpoints.

To deploy ECN or RED, administrators can configure these mechanisms on network devices using CLI commands or through graphical interfaces.

Effective QoS prioritization and mechanisms are essential for ensuring the reliable delivery of critical applications and services in modern networks.

By classifying, policing, shaping, and queuing traffic effectively, network administrators can optimize network performance, reduce latency, and maintain quality for voice, video, and data applications.

QoS techniques should align with the specific requirements and characteristics of the network and its traffic, allowing administrators to strike the right balance between resource utilization and service quality.

In summary, QoS mechanisms and prioritization techniques are invaluable tools for network administrators tasked with managing and optimizing network performance.

Understanding the principles of traffic classification, policing, shaping, and queuing, and how to configure them using CLI commands, empowers administrators to design and maintain networks that meet the demands of diverse applications and ensure a consistent, high-quality user experience.

Traffic policing and shaping are critical Quality of Service (QoS) mechanisms used by network administrators to control and manage the flow of traffic within a network, ensuring that it aligns with the network's capacity and policy objectives.

These techniques are vital in modern networks, where various types of traffic compete for limited resources, and administrators need to prioritize, shape, and control traffic to meet performance and service level requirements.

Traffic policing involves the monitoring and control of network traffic based on predefined policies and rate limits, allowing administrators to enforce specific traffic profiles and manage congestion.

Policing can be particularly useful when network resources are limited or when it's necessary to prevent certain types of traffic from consuming excessive bandwidth.

To configure traffic policing on a router or switch, administrators typically use Command Line Interface (CLI) commands to create policies that define how traffic should be policed.

For example, on a Cisco router, you can create a traffic policy using the following CLI commands:

scssCopy code

```
Router(config)# access-list [access-list number] permit [source] [destination] Router(config)# class-map [class-map name] Router(config-cmap)# match access-group [access-list number] Router(config)# policy-map [policy-map name] Router(config-pmap)# class [class-map name] Router(config-pmap-c)# police [rate] [burst]
```

These commands allow you to create an access control list (ACL) to specify the traffic you want to police, define a class map to match the ACL, create a policy map to apply the policing action, and configure the police command to set the rate and burst size for policing the traffic.

Once configured, the router will enforce the policing policy, either dropping or remarking packets that exceed the specified rate limit, ensuring that network resources are used efficiently.

Traffic shaping, on the other hand, is a QoS technique that smooths the flow of traffic by buffering and delaying packets before they are transmitted.

Shaping helps control bursty traffic and prevent it from overloading network links, resulting in improved network performance and reduced congestion.

To configure traffic shaping on a router or switch, administrators use CLI commands to create shaping policies that determine how traffic should be shaped.

For instance, on a Cisco router, you can create a shaping policy using the following CLI commands:

scssCopy code

Router(config)# policy-map [policy-map name]
Router(config-pmap)# class [class name] Router(config-pmap-c)# shape [average rate] [burst]

These commands allow you to create a policy map, define a class map to match the traffic you want to shape, and configure the shape command to set the desired average rate and burst size for shaping the traffic.

Once shaping is configured, the router will delay the transmission of packets to ensure that they conform to the specified rate, preventing network congestion and maintaining consistent performance.

When deciding between traffic policing and shaping, administrators need to consider their network's requirements and objectives.

Policing is suitable for situations where it is essential to strictly enforce rate limits and discard excess traffic, such as preventing bandwidth abuse or ensuring that specific service-level agreements (SLAs) are met.

Shaping is more appropriate when network traffic needs to be smoothed, ensuring a more even and predictable flow, which is particularly important for real-time applications like voice and video.

In practice, network administrators often combine both traffic policing and shaping to achieve optimal QoS in their networks.

For example, they may use traffic policing to enforce strict rate limits on certain types of traffic, while using shaping to ensure that real-time applications receive a consistent and predictable level of bandwidth.

Additionally, traffic policing and shaping can be applied to different classes of traffic, allowing administrators to prioritize critical applications and control less important traffic.

For example, VoIP traffic can be assigned a higher priority and shaped to ensure low latency, while bulk file transfers may be policed to prevent them from consuming excessive bandwidth.

These techniques are essential in ensuring that networks operate efficiently and deliver a high-quality user experience, especially in environments with diverse traffic patterns and varying QoS requirements.

In summary, traffic policing and shaping are indispensable QoS mechanisms used by network administrators to control and manage the flow of traffic within networks.

Understanding the principles of these techniques and how to configure them using CLI commands empowers administrators to design and maintain networks that meet the demands of different applications, optimize resource utilization, and ensure consistent and predictable network performance.

## Chapter 7: Network Protocols Beyond TCP/IP

Routing Information Protocol (RIP) is one of the oldest and most widely known dynamic routing protocols used in computer networks.

RIP is part of a class of routing protocols called distance-vector protocols, which are used to determine the best path for routing data between routers within a network.

The main goal of RIP is to maintain and distribute routing information among routers so that they can make informed decisions about the optimal path to forward data packets.

RIP operates based on the Bellman-Ford algorithm, which calculates the shortest path to a destination by counting the number of hops (routers) a packet must traverse.

RIP routers periodically exchange routing tables, which contain information about available network destinations and their associated hop counts.

One of the key characteristics of RIP is its simplicity, making it relatively easy to configure and deploy in small to medium-sized networks.

To enable RIP on a Cisco router using Command Line Interface (CLI) commands, administrators typically follow these steps:

Access the router's CLI.

Enter global configuration mode with the **configure terminal** command.

Create a RIP routing process using the **router rip** command.

Specify the networks that should be included in the RIP routing process using the **network [network address]** command.

For example, to enable RIP and include the network 192.168.1.0 in the RIP process, administrators would use the following CLI commands:

arduinoCopy code

```
Router(config)# router rip   Router(config-router)# network 192.168.1.0
```

These commands tell the router to participate in RIP routing and advertise the specified network.

RIP uses a metric called hop count to determine the best path to a destination.

Each router advertises its routing table to its neighbors, and the neighbors update their own tables based on the received information.

Routers use the hop count metric to choose the route with the fewest hops to a destination as the best path.

However, RIP has limitations that make it less suitable for large or complex networks.

One major drawback is its slow convergence time, which is the time it takes for routers to adapt to changes in the network topology.

RIP routers update their routing tables every 30 seconds, which can lead to delays in responding to network changes.

Additionally, RIP has a maximum hop count limit of 15, meaning it cannot route packets to destinations that are more than 15 hops away.

This limitation makes RIP unsuitable for large networks or networks with complex topologies.

To mitigate some of these limitations, a newer version called RIPng (RIP Next Generation) was introduced to support IPv6, offering improvements over traditional RIP.

RIPng uses the same basic principles as RIP but extends them to support IPv6 addressing and routing.

Configuration of RIPng is similar to traditional RIP, with the main difference being the use of IPv6 network addresses and commands.

For example, to enable RIPng on a Cisco router for an IPv6 network, administrators would use commands like these:

scssCopy code

Router(config)# ipv6 unicast-routing Router(config)# router rip Router(config-router)# version 2 Router(config-router)# network [IPv6 network address]

These commands enable RIPng, specify the use of version 2, and include an IPv6 network in the routing process.

In summary, Routing Information Protocol (RIP) is a well-known and widely used distance-vector routing protocol designed to determine the best path for routing data within computer networks.

RIP is relatively simple to configure and deploy, making it suitable for small to medium-sized networks.

However, it has limitations, such as slow convergence and a maximum hop count of 15, which make it less suitable for large or complex networks.

To address some of these limitations, RIPng was introduced to support IPv6 and provide improvements over traditional RIP.

Administrators can use CLI commands to enable and configure RIP or RIPng on network devices, adapting the protocol to their specific network requirements.

The Internet Control Message Protocol for IPv6, abbreviated as ICMPv6, plays a crucial role in the functioning and management of IPv6 networks.

ICMPv6 is the successor to ICMP for IPv4 and provides a set of essential control and error messaging services for IPv6.

One of the primary purposes of ICMPv6 is to facilitate communication between network devices, particularly routers and hosts, by conveying important information about network conditions, errors, and diagnostics.

ICMPv6 serves as the mechanism for routers to communicate with neighboring routers and hosts, ensuring proper routing and addressing within an IPv6 network.

Just like its predecessor ICMP for IPv4, ICMPv6 consists of various message types that serve distinct functions.

One of the most commonly used ICMPv6 message types is the Echo Request and Echo Reply messages, which are similar to ICMP Echo Request (ping) and Echo Reply in IPv4.

These messages enable network administrators to check the reachability and round-trip time to a specific IPv6-enabled device, ensuring that it's responsive and operational.

To send an ICMPv6 Echo Request message from a device's Command Line Interface (CLI), administrators can use a command like this:

cssCopy code

ping6 [IPv6 address]

This command instructs the device to send an ICMPv6 Echo Request to the specified IPv6 address and wait for an Echo Reply.

Another important ICMPv6 message type is the Router Advertisement (RA), which is sent by routers to advertise their presence and configuration information to neighboring hosts.

RA messages contain details such as the router's IPv6 address, network prefix, and various flags and options.

To configure a router to send RA messages on an IPv6 network, administrators typically use CLI commands to specify the advertising parameters.

For instance, on a Cisco router, the following CLI commands enable RA messages on a specific interface:

```
scssCopy code
```
Router(config)# interface [interface name] Router(config-if)# ipv6 nd ra-interval [interval] Router(config-if)# ipv6 nd prefix [prefix]/[prefix length]

These commands set the RA interval and announce an IPv6 prefix, allowing hosts on the network to automatically configure their IPv6 addresses.

ICMPv6 also includes the Neighbor Solicitation (NS) and Neighbor Advertisement (NA) messages, which are vital for the resolution of IPv6 addresses to link-layer (MAC) addresses within a local network segment.

These messages are used by hosts to discover the link-layer addresses of other devices on the same network, such as routers and other hosts.

For example, when a host needs to determine the link-layer address of a router, it sends an NS message, and the router responds with a corresponding NA message.

To illustrate this in CLI commands, consider a scenario where a host wants to resolve the link-layer address of a router:

```
cssCopy code
```
ping6 [IPv6 address]

In this case, the host first sends an ICMPv6 Echo Request message to the router's IPv6 address.

If the router is on the same local network segment, it will respond with an ICMPv6 Echo Reply message.

If the router is not on the same segment, the host will send an NS message to the router's solicited-node multicast address, and the router will respond with an NA message, providing its link-layer address.

Beyond these basic ICMPv6 message types, ICMPv6 includes other messages for functions like path MTU (Maximum Transmission Unit) discovery, multicast listener discovery, and error reporting.

One notable ICMPv6 message type is the Destination Unreachable message, which routers and hosts use to communicate errors when a destination cannot be reached. This message helps diagnose and troubleshoot connectivity issues within an IPv6 network.

To understand how ICMPv6 is instrumental in diagnosing network problems, consider a situation where a host attempts to communicate with a remote server but encounters a routing issue:

cssCopy code

```
ping6 [IPv6 address]
```

In this case, if the router encounters a problem while forwarding the packet to the destination, it will send a Destination Unreachable message back to the host.

The ICMPv6 Destination Unreachable message contains information about the specific issue, helping network administrators identify and resolve the problem.

In summary, the Internet Control Message Protocol for IPv6 (ICMPv6) plays a vital role in the operation and management of IPv6 networks. ICMPv6 messages provide essential functions such as reachability testing, neighbor discovery, router advertisement, and error reporting. By using CLI commands to send and receive ICMPv6 messages, network administrators can diagnose network issues, ensure proper routing, and facilitate communication between IPv6 devices within their networks.

## Chapter 8: Wireless Networking Standards

Wi-Fi standards have evolved significantly over the years, enabling wireless communication to become an integral part of our daily lives.

These standards, defined by the Institute of Electrical and Electronics Engineers (IEEE), establish the specifications for wireless communication in various frequency bands, enabling interoperability between different Wi-Fi devices.

One of the most widely known and used Wi-Fi standards is 802.11, which has seen multiple iterations and improvements over time.

For example, the 802.11ac standard, also known as Wi-Fi 5, brought significant enhancements to wireless networks when it was introduced.

802.11ac operates in the 5 GHz frequency band and introduced features like wider channel widths, multiple spatial streams, and beamforming, allowing for faster data rates and improved coverage.

To configure an access point to use the 802.11ac standard, administrators typically use CLI commands or graphical interfaces provided by the manufacturer.

For instance, on a Cisco access point, you might configure the 802.11ac standard like this:

scssCopy code

AP (config)# wireless-profile policy-profile [profile name]

AP (config-wireless-profile)# 802.11 a AP (config-wireless-profile- 802.11 a)# support 802.11 ac

These commands enable support for 802.11ac on the access point, allowing devices to connect using this standard.

Another significant advancement in Wi-Fi standards is the 802.11ax standard, also known as Wi-Fi 6.

Wi-Fi 6 builds upon the foundation of previous standards and introduces technologies like Orthogonal Frequency Division Multiple Access (OFDMA) and Basic Service Set (BSS) Coloring, which improve network efficiency and reduce interference in dense environments.

To configure an access point for Wi-Fi 6 (802.11ax), administrators would typically use similar CLI commands or graphical interfaces provided by the manufacturer, adapting the configuration to the specific standard and features.

The deployment of Wi-Fi standards involves not only access points but also client devices that must support the same standard to take full advantage of the improvements in speed, reliability, and efficiency.

For example, to benefit from Wi-Fi 6, both the access point and the client devices must be Wi-Fi 6 compatible.

Each Wi-Fi standard defines the modulation and coding schemes used for data transmission, which directly impact the achievable data rates and the ability to handle multiple clients simultaneously.

As Wi-Fi standards advance, they aim to address the growing demands of users for faster and more reliable wireless connectivity.

In addition to 802.11ac and 802.11ax, there are other standards like 802.11n (Wi-Fi 4) and 802.11ad (WiGig) that cater to specific use cases and frequency bands.

For example, 802.11n introduced Multiple Input, Multiple Output (MIMO) technology, which allows multiple antennas on both the transmitter and receiver to improve data rates and signal quality.

802.11ad operates in the 60 GHz frequency band and is designed for short-range, high-speed connections, making it suitable for applications like wireless docking and virtual reality.

The choice of which Wi-Fi standard to deploy depends on various factors, including the specific use case, available devices, and network requirements.

For example, a home network may benefit from the improved coverage and speed of 802.11ax, while an industrial environment might require the specialized capabilities of 802.11ad for low-latency connections.

In addition to these mainstream Wi-Fi standards, there are emerging technologies and standards that aim to push the boundaries of wireless communication further.

For instance, 802.11ay is an upcoming standard designed to operate in the 60 GHz frequency band, offering even higher data rates and potential applications in augmented reality and ultra-high-definition video streaming.

To configure and deploy these emerging standards, administrators will continue to rely on CLI commands or graphical interfaces provided by network equipment manufacturers, adapting their configurations to the specific standard and use case.

In summary, Wi-Fi standards have evolved over time to meet the increasing demands for wireless connectivity.

Standards like 802.11ac and 802.11ax have brought significant improvements in speed and efficiency, while others like 802.11ad target specific niche applications.

The choice of which standard to deploy depends on the specific requirements of the network and the capabilities of the devices involved.

As technology continues to advance, new Wi-Fi standards will continue to emerge, offering even faster and more reliable wireless communication options. Administrators will need to adapt and configure their networks accordingly to stay at the forefront of wireless technology.

Wireless security protocols are fundamental in safeguarding the confidentiality, integrity, and availability of data transmitted over wireless networks.

One of the most significant advancements in recent years is the introduction of Wi-Fi Protected Access 3 (WPA3), which represents a substantial improvement over its predecessor, WPA2.

WPA3 was developed to address vulnerabilities discovered in WPA2 and enhance the overall security of Wi-Fi networks.

To configure and deploy WPA3, network administrators typically use CLI commands or graphical interfaces provided by wireless access points and routers.

For instance, on a Cisco wireless access point, administrators may set up WPA3 using commands like these:

scssCopy code

AP (config)# wlan [WLAN ID] AP (config-wlan)# security wpa3 AP (config-wlan-security-wpa3)# enable

These commands enable WPA3 security for a specific WLAN (Wireless Local Area Network) and ensure that devices connecting to that network use WPA3 for encryption and authentication.

WPA3 offers several key security features that significantly enhance wireless network protection.

One of the standout features is Simultaneous Authentication of Equals (SAE), also known as Dragonfly.

SAE replaces the pre-shared key (PSK) used in WPA2 with a more secure and resilient key exchange mechanism.

In WPA2, an attacker could potentially crack a weak PSK through a brute-force attack, while SAE uses a secure key exchange protocol that is resistant to such attacks.

Another crucial feature of WPA3 is Forward Secrecy, which ensures that even if an attacker captures encrypted traffic and obtains the encryption key in the future, they cannot decrypt past traffic.

This forward secrecy protection adds an additional layer of security, preventing retrospective decryption of previously captured data.

Moreover, WPA3 enhances security for open Wi-Fi networks, which are typically less secure due to their lack of encryption.

WPA3 introduces Opportunistic Wireless Encryption (OWE), also known as Enhanced Open, which encrypts traffic on open networks without requiring a password.

OWE protects users from eavesdropping and ensures that even on open networks, their data remains confidential.

Additionally, WPA3 includes protection against brute-force attacks on the network's PSK.

It employs a mechanism that makes it challenging for attackers to repeatedly guess passwords, making password-based attacks significantly more difficult.

This protection is especially important given the increasing prevalence of powerful computing resources available to attackers.

While WPA3 represents a significant leap forward in wireless security, it's essential to note that not all devices and networks support WPA3.

Many older devices may only support WPA2 or even WPA, and some networks may continue to use these older standards.

As a result, network administrators often need to configure their networks to support multiple security protocols, allowing a range of devices to connect securely.

To do this, administrators can typically use CLI commands or graphical interfaces to configure multiple security profiles on their access points or routers, each supporting different security protocols.

For example, on a Cisco wireless access point, they might configure multiple security profiles like this:

scssCopy code

```
AP(config)# wlan [WLAN ID] AP(config-wlan)# security wpa2 AP(config-wlan-security-wpa2)# enable AP(config-wlan)# wlan [WLAN ID] AP(config-wlan)# security wpa3 AP(config-wlan-security-wpa3)# enable
```

These commands create separate WLANs with different security protocols, allowing devices to choose the appropriate one based on their capabilities.

In summary, wireless security protocols like WPA3 are essential for protecting the confidentiality and integrity of data transmitted over Wi-Fi networks.

WPA3 offers significant improvements in security, including SAE, forward secrecy, and protection against brute-force attacks.

However, it's crucial for network administrators to understand that not all devices and networks support WPA3, necessitating the configuration of multiple security profiles to accommodate different security standards.

By deploying the right security protocols and keeping their networks up to date, administrators can ensure the continued security of their wireless communications in an ever-evolving threat landscape.

## Chapter 9: Virtual Private Networks (VPNs)

Virtual Private Networks, or VPNs, have become an integral part of modern network infrastructure, providing secure and private communication over public networks like the internet.

A VPN creates a secure tunnel that encrypts data as it travels between a user's device and a remote server or network.

There are various VPN types and deployment models, each designed to meet specific security, scalability, and accessibility requirements.

One of the most common VPN types is the Site-to-Site VPN, which is commonly used in enterprise networks to securely connect multiple remote sites or branch offices.

To configure a Site-to-Site VPN, network administrators typically use CLI commands or a graphical interface provided by network devices such as routers or firewalls.

For example, on a Cisco router, administrators might configure a Site-to-Site VPN like this:

```
scssCopy code
Router(config)# crypto isakmp policy 1 Router(config-isakmp)# encryption aes Router(config-isakmp)# hash sha256 Router(config-isakmp)# authentication pre-share Router(config-isakmp)# group 14 Router(config-isakmp)# exit Router(config)# crypto isakmp key [pre-shared key] address [peer IP address] Router(config)# crypto ipsec transform-set [transform set name] esp-aes esp-sha256-hmac Router(config)# crypto map [crypto map name] 10 ipsec-isakmp Router(config-crypto-map)# set peer [peer IP address] Router(config-crypto-map)# set transform-set
```

[transform set name]  Router(config-crypto-map)# match address [access-list name]  Router(config-crypto-map)# exit Router(config)# interface [interface name]  Router(config-if)# crypto map [crypto map name]

These commands configure a Site-to-Site VPN using the Internet Security Association and Key Management Protocol (ISAKMP) and the IPsec protocol suite, ensuring secure communication between the two sites.

Another widely used VPN type is the Remote Access VPN, which allows remote users or devices to securely connect to a corporate network from anywhere with internet access.

To deploy a Remote Access VPN, network administrators may use VPN client software on the remote device, and they typically configure VPN server settings on a VPN concentrator or firewall.

For instance, on a Cisco VPN concentrator, administrators may configure Remote Access VPN settings like this:
scssCopy code

Concentrator(config)#  crypto  isakmp  policy  10 Concentrator(config-isakmp)#  authentication  pre-share Concentrator(config-isakmp)#  encryption  aes Concentrator(config-isakmp)#  hash  sha256 Concentrator(config-isakmp)#  group  14 Concentrator(config-isakmp)# exit  Concentrator(config)# crypto isakmp client configuration group [group name] Concentrator(config-isakmp-group)# key [pre-shared key] Concentrator(config-isakmp-group)# pool [VPN pool name] Concentrator(config-isakmp-group)# acl [access-list name] Concentrator(config-isakmp-group)#  save-password Concentrator(config-isakmp-group)# max-users [maximum number of users]  Concentrator(config-isakmp-group)# exit

Concentrator (config)# interface [interface name] Concentrator (config-if)# ip address [VPN interface IP address] Concentrator (config-if)# crypto map [crypto map name]

These commands configure a Remote Access VPN using ISAKMP and IPsec, allowing remote users to establish secure connections to the corporate network.

Apart from these common VPN types, there are other specialized VPNs such as SSL VPNs, which use the Secure Sockets Layer (SSL) or Transport Layer Security (TLS) protocols to provide secure remote access.

To deploy an SSL VPN, administrators typically configure settings on an SSL VPN gateway or appliance and provide users with web-based access to network resources.

For example, setting up an SSL VPN on a Cisco ASA firewall might involve configuring SSL settings and user authentication methods through a graphical interface.

Point-to-Point Protocol (PPP) over Ethernet (PPPoE) is another VPN deployment model often used by Internet Service Providers (ISPs) to provide secure connectivity to residential customers.

PPPoE combines PPP authentication with Ethernet encapsulation, allowing users to connect securely to their ISP's network using a username and password.

To deploy PPPoE, ISPs configure PPPoE servers on their network equipment and provide customers with PPPoE client settings for their routers or modem-router combinations.

For example, on a DSL modem-router, users might configure PPPoE settings using a web-based interface by entering their username and password provided by the ISP.

While VPNs offer various deployment models and types, it's essential to choose the one that best fits the organization's needs, security requirements, and network topology.

Administrators must consider factors like scalability, accessibility, and the level of control they need over the VPN.

Additionally, the choice of VPN technology may influence the hardware and software used, as different VPN types may require specific devices or software clients.

In summary, VPNs play a vital role in ensuring secure and private communication over public networks like the internet.

There are various VPN types, including Site-to-Site VPNs and Remote Access VPNs, each with its configuration methods and deployment models.

Network administrators must carefully select and configure the appropriate VPN type to meet the organization's specific requirements, ensuring the confidentiality and integrity of data transmitted over their networks.


VPN encryption and authentication are fundamental components of Virtual Private Networks, providing the security necessary to protect data as it traverses public networks.

Encryption is the process of converting plaintext data into ciphertext, rendering it unintelligible to unauthorized parties.

In VPNs, encryption ensures that data transmitted between a user's device and a VPN server or another remote endpoint remains confidential and secure.

To configure encryption in a VPN, administrators typically use cryptographic algorithms and keys.

For example, they might configure the Advanced Encryption Standard (AES) with a 256-bit key, a strong and widely adopted encryption algorithm known for its security.

CLI commands used to configure AES encryption might look like this:

arduinoCopy code

```
crypto ipsec transform-set my-transform-set esp-aes 256
esp-sha256-hmac
```

These commands set up an IPsec transform set using AES encryption with a 256-bit key and the SHA-256 HMAC (Hash-based Message Authentication Code) for data integrity.

Another crucial aspect of VPN security is authentication, which verifies the identities of communicating parties.

Authentication ensures that the devices or users connecting to the VPN are who they claim to be, preventing unauthorized access.

A commonly used authentication method in VPNs is the pre-shared key (PSK).

In this method, both the client and the VPN server share a secret key, which they use to authenticate each other during the connection setup.

CLI commands for configuring PSK authentication might include:

cssCopy code

```
crypto isakmp key [pre-shared key] address [peer IP
address]
```

These commands set up a pre-shared key for Internet Security Association and Key Management Protocol (ISAKMP) authentication between the client and the VPN server.

Alternatively, some VPNs use digital certificates for authentication.

Certificates provide a more robust and scalable authentication method, especially in large enterprise environments.

To configure certificate-based authentication, administrators must generate and distribute certificates to VPN clients and servers.

For example, in a Cisco VPN, administrators might use commands like:

perlCopy code

```
crypto pki trustpoint my-trustpoint enrollment selfsigned
rsakeypair my-keypair
```

These commands create a trustpoint, generate a self-signed certificate, and create an RSA key pair for certificate-based authentication.

Certificate-based authentication offers stronger security than PSKs and is suitable for scenarios where identity verification is critical.

In addition to encryption and authentication, VPNs often incorporate data integrity checks to ensure that data remains unaltered during transmission.

One common method for data integrity is using HMACs, as mentioned earlier, which involves hashing the data and attaching a cryptographic checksum.

For example, to configure data integrity checks using SHA-256 HMAC, administrators might use CLI commands like these:

arduinoCopy code

```
crypto ipsec transform-set my-transform-set esp-aes 256
esp-sha256-hmac
```

These commands configure IPsec to use AES encryption and SHA-256 HMAC for data integrity.

Furthermore, VPNs can employ Perfect Forward Secrecy (PFS) mechanisms to enhance security.

PFS ensures that even if an attacker compromises the private key of one VPN session, they cannot decrypt past or future sessions.

In a Cisco VPN, administrators might enable PFS using CLI commands:

arduinoCopy code

```
crypto map [crypto map name] 10 ipsec-isakmp set pfs
group [DH group]
```

These commands enable PFS for an IPsec policy, specifying a Diffie-Hellman (DH) group for key exchange.

VPN encryption and authentication are critical components in protecting data as it traverses public networks.

Administrators must carefully choose encryption algorithms, authentication methods, and data integrity mechanisms that meet the organization's security requirements.

Furthermore, configuring and managing these security features often involves a combination of CLI commands and graphical interfaces, ensuring that VPNs remain secure and reliable.

By understanding and implementing strong encryption, robust authentication, and data integrity checks, network administrators can create VPNs that safeguard sensitive data against unauthorized access and eavesdropping.

## Chapter 10: Network Troubleshooting and Analysis

Network monitoring and diagnostic tools are essential components of modern network management, providing administrators with the means to oversee network performance, detect issues, and troubleshoot problems effectively.

These tools come in various forms, ranging from simple command-line utilities to sophisticated graphical interfaces, and they play a crucial role in maintaining the reliability and efficiency of networks.

One common category of network monitoring tools is packet analyzers, also known as network protocol analyzers or packet sniffers.

These tools capture and inspect data packets as they traverse the network, allowing administrators to examine the content of packets and identify any anomalies or issues.

A widely used command-line packet analyzer is Wireshark, which provides a comprehensive set of features for capturing, analyzing, and visualizing network traffic.

To capture packets using Wireshark, administrators can use the following CLI command:

cssCopy code

```
wireshark -i [interface name]
```

This command starts Wireshark in live capture mode on the specified network interface, enabling administrators to observe packet traffic in real-time.

Another essential network monitoring tool category is network performance monitoring (NPM) software.

NPM tools continuously collect data about network performance parameters such as bandwidth usage, latency, and packet loss.

These tools help administrators identify performance bottlenecks, plan network capacity upgrades, and optimize network configurations.

One example of an NPM tool is SolarWinds Network Performance Monitor, which offers a web-based interface for monitoring network performance metrics.

To deploy this tool, administrators typically install it on a dedicated server and configure device credentials and monitoring settings through its web interface.

Furthermore, network diagnostic tools assist administrators in troubleshooting network issues and identifying the root causes of problems.

One such tool is the ping command, available in the command-line interface of most operating systems.

To check the reachability of a network device, administrators can use the ping command as follows:

cssCopy code

ping [destination IP address or hostname]

This command sends ICMP (Internet Control Message Protocol) echo request packets to the specified destination and reports whether responses are received.

Another diagnostic tool is the traceroute command, which helps administrators trace the route that packets take from the source to the destination.

The CLI command for traceroute might look like this:

cssCopy code

traceroute [destination IP address or hostname]

Traceroute sends packets with increasing TTL (Time to Live) values to determine the path they take through routers and switches, providing valuable information about network topology and potential trouble spots.

Additionally, network scanning tools are crucial for assessing network security and identifying potential vulnerabilities.

Tools like Nmap (Network Mapper) can scan network devices to discover open ports, running services, and operating systems.

Administrators can use the CLI to initiate a basic Nmap scan with a command like this:

cssCopy code

nmap [target IP address or hostname]

This command initiates a default Nmap scan, providing information about open ports and services on the target device.

Network monitoring and diagnostic tools are not limited to the command line; many of them offer graphical user interfaces (GUIs) for easier configuration and visualization.

For instance, the Nagios Core monitoring system provides a web-based interface for setting up and managing network monitoring tasks.

Administrators can configure host and service checks, define notification policies, and view real-time status updates through the Nagios web interface.

In addition to these tools, SNMP (Simple Network Management Protocol) plays a critical role in network monitoring by enabling the collection of management data from network devices.

Administrators can use SNMP to monitor device performance, track resource utilization, and trigger alerts when predefined thresholds are exceeded.

To enable SNMP on network devices like routers and switches, administrators typically configure SNMP settings using CLI commands or web-based interfaces.

For instance, on a Cisco router, administrators can configure SNMP with commands like these:

cssCopy code

snmp-server community [community string] RO snmp-server host [SNMP manager IP address] [SNMP manager community string]

These commands define an SNMP community string for read-only access and specify the IP address of the SNMP manager that will receive SNMP traps and notifications.

Furthermore, network flow analysis tools are valuable for understanding network traffic patterns and optimizing network performance.

Flow analysis tools like NetFlow and sFlow collect data about traffic flows, including source and destination IP addresses, ports, and data volume.

Administrators can use this data to identify bandwidth hogs, detect abnormal traffic patterns, and plan network improvements.

To enable NetFlow on Cisco routers, administrators can use CLI commands like these:

cssCopy code

interface [interface name] ip flow ingress ip flow egress

These commands configure NetFlow data collection on a specific interface, allowing administrators to analyze traffic statistics using NetFlow analysis tools.

In summary, network monitoring and diagnostic tools are indispensable for effectively managing and troubleshooting modern networks.

They encompass a wide range of utilities, from packet analyzers and performance monitors to diagnostic commands and scanning tools.

These tools, whether deployed through the command line or user-friendly interfaces, empower administrators to maintain network reliability, security, and performance.

Advanced troubleshooting scenarios in networking often

require a deep understanding of network protocols, hardware, and software configurations, as well as the ability to analyze complex issues that may not have obvious solutions.

In these scenarios, network administrators encounter problems that go beyond basic connectivity issues and require a systematic approach to identify and resolve.

For instance, when dealing with intermittent network outages, administrators may need to conduct packet captures to analyze traffic patterns and pinpoint the source of the problem.

To capture packets on a specific interface of a Cisco router, administrators can use the following CLI command:

arduinoCopy code

```
monitor capture buffer [buffer name] size [size in MB]
monitor capture buffer [buffer name] filter [access-list]
monitor capture point ip cef [point name] gi0/0 both
monitor capture point associate [point name] [buffer name]
monitor capture point start [point name]
```

These commands configure packet capturing by creating a buffer, specifying an access list for filtering, associating the capture point with an interface, and starting the capture process.

Packet captures can provide valuable insights into network anomalies, such as unexpected traffic spikes or unusual packet behaviors.

Another advanced troubleshooting scenario involves resolving routing issues in a complex network topology.

For example, when dealing with routing loops or incorrect routing table entries, administrators may need to verify routing protocols, redistribute routes, or adjust route metrics.

To troubleshoot routing issues in a Cisco environment, administrators can use the following CLI commands:

sqlCopy code

show ip route show ip protocols show ip ospf neighbor show ip bgp summary

These commands provide information about the current routing table, routing protocols, OSPF neighbor relationships, and BGP (Border Gateway Protocol) summary.

By examining this data and comparing it to the expected network topology, administrators can identify and rectify routing problems.

In advanced scenarios, network administrators may encounter security breaches or unauthorized access attempts.

In such cases, administrators must investigate the incident, analyze logs, and implement security measures to prevent future breaches.

To investigate a security incident, administrators can use CLI commands like these:

sqlCopy code

show access-list show crypto isakmp sa show ip nat translations show aaa authentication

These commands display information about access control lists (ACLs), VPN (Virtual Private Network) tunnels, NAT (Network Address Translation) translations, and AAA (Authentication, Authorization, and Accounting) authentication.

By examining these logs and configurations, administrators can trace the source of security breaches and take appropriate actions, such as adjusting firewall rules or updating authentication policies.

Moreover, in complex network environments, administrators may encounter issues related to Quality of

Service (QoS), affecting the performance of critical applications.

To troubleshoot QoS problems, administrators can use CLI commands to verify QoS policies and traffic classification.

For instance, in a Cisco router, administrators can use these commands:

goCopy code

show policy-map show class-map show policy-map interface [interface name]

These commands provide information about configured QoS policies, class maps, and the application of QoS policies on specific interfaces.

Analyzing this data allows administrators to ensure that QoS policies are correctly applied and prioritize traffic appropriately.

Advanced troubleshooting scenarios can also involve diagnosing network performance degradation attributed to device resource constraints.

For example, when dealing with high CPU or memory utilization on network devices, administrators must identify the root cause and take remedial actions.

To diagnose resource utilization issues in a Cisco router, administrators can use CLI commands like these:

sqlCopy code

show processes cpu sorted show memory show interfaces | include (line protocol | input rate | output rate)

These commands display CPU utilization, memory usage, and interface statistics, helping administrators identify resource-intensive processes or interfaces.

Administrators can then optimize configurations or upgrade hardware components as needed to address resource constraints.

Furthermore, administrators may encounter challenges related to VLAN (Virtual LAN) configurations and trunking issues.

In advanced troubleshooting scenarios, identifying and resolving VLAN-related problems requires a thorough understanding of VLAN configurations and switch behavior.

To troubleshoot VLAN issues in a Cisco switch, administrators can use CLI commands like these:

sqlCopy code

```
show vlan show interface trunk show mac address-table
show spanning-tree vlan [VLAN ID]
```

These commands provide information about VLAN configurations, trunking status, MAC address tables, and Spanning Tree Protocol (STP) settings.

By analyzing this data and comparing it to the expected VLAN configuration, administrators can address VLAN-related issues.

Finally, advanced troubleshooting scenarios often involve complex interactions between different network technologies and protocols.

For example, administrators may need to diagnose problems at the intersection of VPNs and routing protocols, where misconfigurations can lead to routing inconsistencies.

To troubleshoot such scenarios, administrators must have a deep understanding of both VPN and routing technologies.

They can use CLI commands like these to investigate VPN and routing interactions:

sqlCopy code

```
show crypto isakmp sa show crypto ipsec sa show ip route
show ip ospf neighbor
```

These commands provide information about VPN tunnel status, routing tables, and OSPF neighbor relationships, allowing administrators to diagnose issues related to route distribution over VPN tunnels.

In summary, advanced troubleshooting scenarios in networking demand a combination of in-depth knowledge, practical experience, and the ability to use CLI commands effectively.

Administrators must be prepared to tackle a wide range of complex issues, from intermittent network outages to security breaches, resource constraints, QoS problems, VLAN misconfigurations, and complex interactions between network technologies.

A systematic and methodical approach, along with the use of appropriate CLI commands, is essential to diagnose and resolve these challenging network problems effectively.

## BOOK 3
## ADVANCED TCP/IP AND CAMPUS LAN SWITCHING

### ROB BOTWRIGHT

## Chapter 1: Advanced TCP/IP Protocols and Techniques

Advanced transport layer protocols are crucial components of modern networking, facilitating the reliable and efficient transfer of data across networks while offering features and capabilities beyond what basic transport protocols provide.

One such advanced transport layer protocol is the Transmission Control Protocol (TCP), which remains the foundation of reliable data transmission on the internet.

TCP offers a comprehensive set of features, including error checking, flow control, congestion control, and data sequencing, to ensure data arrives intact and in the correct order.

To establish a TCP connection, the client and server perform a three-way handshake, a process initiated by the client sending a SYN packet to the server, the server responding with a SYN-ACK packet, and the client confirming with an ACK packet.

The simplicity and effectiveness of TCP have made it the go-to protocol for applications that require guaranteed data delivery, such as web browsing, email, and file transfer.

Another advanced transport layer protocol is the User Datagram Protocol (UDP), which provides a lightweight and connectionless transport service.

Unlike TCP, UDP does not establish a connection or guarantee data delivery, making it faster but less reliable.

UDP is commonly used for applications where real-time data transmission is critical, such as video streaming, online gaming, and VoIP (Voice over IP).

To initiate a UDP session, applications simply send data packets without the overhead of establishing and maintaining a connection, making it well-suited for scenarios where low latency is more important than error recovery.

In addition to TCP and UDP, there are several other advanced transport layer protocols, each tailored to specific use cases and requirements.

For instance, the Datagram Congestion Control Protocol (DCCP) is designed for applications that need congestion control without the overhead of TCP.

DCCP provides features like congestion control and flow-based communication, making it suitable for real-time multimedia applications and online gaming.

To deploy DCCP, applications need to implement the DCCP protocol stack and use appropriate socket API calls to establish and manage DCCP connections.

Stream Control Transmission Protocol (SCTP) is another advanced transport protocol that combines the reliability of TCP with the message-oriented nature of UDP.

SCTP is particularly useful for applications that require reliable data delivery while supporting multiple streams and minimizing head-of-line blocking.

To use SCTP, applications need to implement the SCTP protocol stack and use socket API calls to create and manage SCTP associations and streams.

Moreover, the QUIC (Quick UDP Internet Connections) protocol is an emerging transport layer protocol developed by Google to address the limitations of TCP and improve web performance.

QUIC is designed to reduce latency and improve security by encrypting data from the outset and multiplexing multiple streams over a single connection.

To implement QUIC, applications need to use libraries or frameworks that support the protocol, as it operates over UDP.

Furthermore, Multipath TCP (MPTCP) is an advanced transport protocol that enables a single connection to utilize multiple network paths simultaneously, providing redundancy and improved throughput.

MPTCP is particularly valuable in scenarios where network paths may be unreliable or congested.

To deploy MPTCP, both the client and server need to support the protocol, and administrators should configure network equipment to allow MPTCP traffic.

Additionally, the WebSocket protocol is an advanced transport layer protocol that enables bidirectional, full-duplex communication over a single TCP connection.

WebSockets are commonly used in web applications to provide real-time interactions between clients and servers.

To use WebSockets, developers implement the WebSocket protocol in their web applications and establish WebSocket connections using JavaScript or other client-side technologies.

Furthermore, the Border Gateway Protocol (BGP) is an advanced transport protocol used to exchange routing and reachability information between autonomous systems on the internet.

BGP is critical for the proper functioning of the global internet, as it determines the path that data takes between networks.

To configure BGP, network administrators use CLI commands to define BGP neighbors, specify routing policies, and manage route advertisements.

In summary, advanced transport layer protocols play a crucial role in modern networking, offering a wide range of features and capabilities to support various applications and requirements.

TCP remains the foundation of reliable data transmission, while UDP provides low-latency communication for real-time applications.

Other protocols like DCCP, SCTP, QUIC, MPTCP, WebSocket, and BGP cater to specific use cases and networking scenarios, each requiring unique deployment and configuration methods.

Understanding these advanced transport layer protocols is essential for network administrators and developers to choose the right protocol for their applications and ensure optimal performance and reliability.

Implementing an IPsec (Internet Protocol Security) VPN (Virtual Private Network) is a fundamental and essential aspect of network security that allows organizations to secure data transmission over untrusted networks.

IPsec VPNs provide a robust framework for encrypting and authenticating data, ensuring confidentiality, integrity, and authenticity in network communications.

To begin the implementation of an IPsec VPN, one of the primary considerations is selecting the appropriate IPsec protocol suite, which typically consists of two key components: the Authentication Header (AH) and the Encapsulating Security Payload (ESP).

The AH protocol provides authentication and integrity without encryption, while the ESP protocol offers both encryption and authentication.

The choice between these protocols depends on the specific security requirements of the VPN deployment.

To implement IPsec, administrators need to configure VPN endpoints, which are typically routers or security appliances that support IPsec functionality.

Configuring an IPsec VPN on a Cisco router, for example, involves using CLI commands to define various parameters, including:

cssCopy code

crypto isakmp policy [policy number] encryption [encryption algorithm] hash [hash algorithm] authentication pre-share group [Diffie-Hellman group]

These commands establish the ISAKMP (Internet Security Association and Key Management Protocol) policy, which defines the negotiation parameters for the VPN connection.

Next, administrators configure the pre-shared keys for authentication:

cssCopy code

crypto isakmp key [key] address [peer address]

This command specifies the pre-shared key and associates it with the remote peer's IP address.

To configure the actual IPsec transform sets that define encryption and authentication algorithms, the following CLI commands are used:

cssCopy code

crypto ipsec transform-set [name] [encryption algorithm] [encryption key] [authentication algorithm] [authentication key]

These commands define the encryption and authentication methods used to secure the data.

Once the transform sets are defined, administrators create crypto maps to specify how traffic should be encrypted and authenticated:

cssCopy code

crypto map [map name] [sequence number] ipsec-isakmp description [description] set peer [peer address] set transform-set [transform set name] match address [access list]

These commands associate the crypto map with the remote peer, specify the transform set to use, and define the access list that identifies the traffic to be protected.

To apply the crypto map to an interface, administrators use the following command:

goCopy code

interface [interface name] crypto map [map name]

This command associates the crypto map with the specific interface, allowing traffic to be encrypted and authenticated according to the configured policy.

Furthermore, when implementing an IPsec VPN, it's essential to define the access control policies that determine which traffic is allowed through the VPN tunnel.

Access control lists (ACLs) are typically used to permit or deny traffic based on source and destination IP addresses, ports, and protocols.

For example, to create an ACL that permits traffic from a specific source to a specific destination, administrators can use commands like:

cssCopy code

access-list [number] permit ip [source] [source mask] [destination] [destination mask]

This command specifies the source and destination IP addresses and their corresponding masks.

Once the ACL is defined, it can be referenced in the crypto map configuration to determine which traffic should be encrypted and sent through the VPN tunnel.

Additionally, IPsec VPN implementations often involve the use of VPN tunnels between multiple remote sites, creating a hub-and-spoke or meshed network topology.

In such scenarios, administrators need to configure VPN tunnels on all participating devices, ensuring consistent policies and parameters.

To configure a remote site's router as a VPN endpoint, administrators can use the same set of CLI commands mentioned earlier.

However, they should ensure that the policies, pre-shared keys, transform sets, and access control lists match those configured on the central VPN gateway.

Furthermore, IPsec VPN implementations may require additional considerations, such as NAT (Network Address Translation) traversal, to ensure that VPN traffic can traverse NAT devices without issues.

NAT traversal techniques like UDP encapsulation (UDP-ESP) or the use of NAT-T (NAT Traversal) protocols can be employed to address NAT-related challenges.

To enable NAT traversal on a Cisco router, administrators can use the following command:

cssCopy code

```
crypto isakmp nat-traversal [nat traversal method]
```

This command configures the router to use NAT traversal mechanisms when communicating with peers that are located behind NAT devices.

Moreover, the deployment of IPsec VPNs often involves the use of digital certificates or other authentication methods, such as RADIUS (Remote Authentication Dial-In User Service), for user and device authentication.

For example, to configure a Cisco router to use digital certificates for authentication, administrators can execute the following CLI commands:

cssCopy code

```
crypto key generate rsa general-keys modulus [modulus size] crypto pki trustpoint [trustpoint name] enrollment
```

selfsigned subject-name [subject name] revocation-check none

These commands generate a self-signed RSA key pair, create a trustpoint for certificate enrollment, specify the subject name, and disable certificate revocation checks.

Finally, administrators can enroll devices for digital certificates using the command:

cssCopy code

crypto pki enroll [trustpoint name]

This command initiates the enrollment process, generating and installing the digital certificate on the device.

In summary, the implementation of an IPsec VPN involves a series of critical steps, including the selection of appropriate IPsec protocols, the configuration of VPN endpoints, the definition of access control policies, and considerations for NAT traversal and authentication methods.

Understanding how to use CLI commands to configure and manage IPsec VPNs is essential for network administrators responsible for securing data communications over untrusted networks.

## Chapter 2: Scaling IP Networks

Hierarchical network design is a structured approach to organizing and planning a network infrastructure that aims to optimize performance, scalability, and manageability.

This design methodology breaks down the network into multiple layers, each with specific functions and responsibilities.

The primary benefit of a hierarchical network design is that it simplifies network management and troubleshooting by creating well-defined boundaries and responsibilities for each layer.

At the core of a hierarchical network design is the concept of network layers, which are typically organized into three main layers: the core layer, distribution layer, and access layer.

The core layer is responsible for high-speed data forwarding and routing within the network, typically using technologies like high-speed routers and redundant links to ensure high availability and minimal latency.

CLI commands to configure the core layer often involve setting up routing protocols like OSPF or BGP, as well as configuring link aggregation for redundancy.

The distribution layer acts as an intermediary between the core and access layers, providing functions such as routing between VLANs, access control, and policy enforcement.

Configuration commands at the distribution layer may include setting up access control lists (ACLs), implementing Quality of Service (QoS) policies, and configuring Virtual LANs (VLANs) to segment network traffic.

The access layer is the point where end devices like computers, printers, and IP phones connect to the network.

It's responsible for user access, device connectivity, and often includes features like Power over Ethernet (PoE) for powering IP phones and other devices.

At the access layer, administrators may use CLI commands to configure port security, VLAN assignment, and PoE settings on network switches.

Hierarchical network design also emphasizes the use of modularization, which means that network components and services are divided into discrete modules, making it easier to add or upgrade specific functions without affecting the entire network.

For example, a network might have separate modules for voice services, data services, and security services, each with its own set of configurations and CLI commands.

Modularization allows for flexibility and scalability as network needs change over time.

Another key concept in hierarchical network design is redundancy, which involves having backup components or paths to ensure network availability in case of failure.

At the core layer, administrators often configure High Availability (HA) features using CLI commands to ensure that if one core router or switch fails, another can seamlessly take over.

In the distribution layer, redundancy can be achieved through technologies like Hot Standby Router Protocol (HSRP) or Virtual Router Redundancy Protocol (VRRP).

These protocols use CLI commands to set up active and standby routers, ensuring network continuity.

Additionally, at the access layer, network switches can be configured with features like EtherChannel or Spanning Tree Protocol (STP) for link redundancy.

As networks continue to grow and evolve, scalability becomes a crucial consideration in hierarchical network design.

Administrators can use CLI commands to configure features like Virtual PortChannels (vPC) in Cisco environments or Link Aggregation Groups (LAG) in other vendor networks to scale the distribution layer and provide additional redundancy.

Security is another paramount aspect of hierarchical network design.

At each layer, administrators must implement security measures to protect against unauthorized access, data breaches, and other threats.

This often involves using CLI commands to configure firewalls, intrusion detection systems, and access control policies.

Segmentation of network traffic through VLANs and ACLs is also critical for enforcing security policies.

Furthermore, monitoring and management are essential components of a hierarchical network design.

Administrators can use CLI commands to configure network management protocols like Simple Network Management Protocol (SNMP) or implement network monitoring tools to keep track of network performance and security.

These tools help in identifying and addressing issues promptly.

Lastly, documentation is a crucial aspect of hierarchical network design.

Administrators should maintain detailed records of configurations, CLI commands, and network diagrams to ensure that the network can be effectively managed and troubleshooted.

Proper documentation helps in maintaining consistency and assists in diagnosing and resolving network problems.

In summary, hierarchical network design is a structured approach to building and organizing network infrastructures that optimize performance, scalability, and manageability.

It involves breaking down the network into layers, implementing redundancy and security measures, and ensuring scalability and efficient management through modularization.

CLI commands play a significant role in configuring and managing various aspects of a hierarchical network, from routing and VLANs to security and redundancy.

With the right design and proper implementation, hierarchical network designs can provide reliable and efficient network infrastructures for organizations of all sizes.

IP addressing and subnet planning for large networks is a complex and critical task that requires careful consideration of address allocation, scalability, and efficient utilization of IP resources.

In large networks, it's essential to design a robust addressing scheme that accommodates the potential growth of devices and subnets while minimizing IP address wastage.

One commonly used approach in large networks is to use Classless Inter-Domain Routing (CIDR) and Variable Length Subnet Masking (VLSM) techniques to allocate IP addresses efficiently.

CIDR allows for the aggregation of IP addresses into larger blocks, reducing the number of routes in the network's routing tables and improving routing efficiency.

To implement CIDR, network administrators can use CLI commands to configure route summarization on routers, grouping contiguous IP addresses into a single, summarized route.

For example, the following CLI command on a Cisco router defines a summarized route:

Copy code

```
ip route 192.168.0.0 255.255.0.0 Null0
```

This command aggregates all IP addresses within the 192.168.0.0/16 range into a single route, reducing the size of the routing table.

VLSM, on the other hand, allows for the allocation of subnets with different subnet masks within the same IP address range.

This technique is particularly useful in large networks where various subnets may have different size requirements.

To implement VLSM, administrators can use CLI commands to define subnets with their respective subnet masks.

For example, in a large network, administrators might configure subnets like this:

scssCopy code

192.168.1.0/24 (Subnet A) 192.168.2.0/25 (Subnet B) 192.168.2.128/26 (Subnet C)

Each subnet uses a different subnet mask based on its specific requirements, allowing for efficient IP address allocation.

Large networks often employ Private IP Addressing, using reserved address ranges like 10.0.0.0/8, 172.16.0.0/12, and 192.168.0.0/16 to allocate internal addresses.

CLI commands can be used to configure these address ranges on routers and switches within the network.

For example, to configure a Cisco router with a range of private IP addresses, administrators can use the following CLI commands:

cssCopy code

ip address 10.0.0.1 255.0.0.0

These commands assign an IP address within the 10.0.0.0/8 range to the router's interface.

In large networks, it's crucial to plan for IP address growth and allocation of addresses to different departments, segments, or geographic locations.

Subnetting and VLANs (Virtual LANs) play a vital role in this planning process.

Administrators can use CLI commands to create and manage VLANs on switches, ensuring that devices within the same VLAN share the same broadcast domain.

For example, to create a VLAN on a Cisco switch, administrators can use commands like:

Copy code

```
vlan 10 name Engineering
```

These commands define VLAN 10 as the "Engineering" VLAN, allowing devices in that VLAN to communicate directly.

To assign VLANs to specific switch ports, administrators can use CLI commands like:

kotlinCopy code

```
interface GigabitEthernet0/1 switchport mode access
switchport access vlan 10
```

These commands configure a switch port to be in access mode and assign it to VLAN 10, allowing devices connected to that port to be part of the Engineering VLAN.

IP address management (IPAM) tools and spreadsheets can also be used to track IP address allocations and ensure efficient utilization.

These tools help administrators keep records of allocated addresses, subnet utilization, and available IP space, reducing the chances of IP address conflicts.

In large networks, the use of DHCP (Dynamic Host Configuration Protocol) is common to automate IP address assignments to devices.

Administrators can configure DHCP servers using CLI commands to define address pools, lease durations, and other parameters.

For instance, to configure a DHCP server on a Cisco router, administrators can use commands like:

arduinoCopy code

```
ip dhcp pool LAN network 192.168.1.0 255.255.255.0
default-router 192.168.1.1
```

These commands create a DHCP pool for the 192.168.1.0/24 subnet, specifying the network range and the default gateway address.

Moreover, IPv6 adoption is becoming increasingly important in large networks due to the exhaustion of IPv4 addresses.

Administrators can use CLI commands to configure IPv6 addresses and subnets on routers and switches, following similar principles of subnet planning and allocation as with IPv4.

For instance, to assign an IPv6 address to an interface on a Cisco router, administrators can use commands like:

kotlinCopy code

```
interface        GigabitEthernet0/0        ipv6        address
2001:db8:1:1::1/64
```

These commands assign an IPv6 address to the interface within the specified subnet.

In summary, IP addressing and subnet planning for large networks require careful consideration of CIDR, VLSM, private IP addressing, VLANs, DHCP, and IPv6 adoption.

Administrators can use CLI commands to configure routers, switches, and DHCP servers, ensuring efficient IP address allocation, management, and scalability in a dynamic network environment.

## Chapter 3: Routing Protocols and Advanced Routing Concepts

BGP (Border Gateway Protocol) is a sophisticated and widely used routing protocol that plays a critical role in the functioning of the Internet and large-scale networks.

To configure BGP successfully, administrators must understand its principles, configuration parameters, and best practices.

One of the fundamental concepts in BGP is the autonomous system (AS), a collection of IP networks and routers under the control of a single organization.

To configure BGP, you need to assign an AS number to your network, which can be obtained from a regional Internet registry (RIR).

For instance, to assign an AS number (e.g., AS 65535) to your network on a Cisco router, you would use a command like this:

Copy code

```
router bgp 65535
```

This command enters the BGP configuration mode with the specified AS number.

Once you've defined your AS number, the next step is to establish BGP peer connections with neighboring routers.

BGP peers exchange routing information, and this exchange is crucial for the protocol's operation.

To configure a BGP peer on a Cisco router, you would typically use commands like:

csharpCopy code

```
neighbor 192.168.1.1 remote-as 65000
```

This command establishes a BGP neighbor relationship with the router at IP address 192.168.1.1, which is in AS 65000.

Authentication can also be enabled between BGP peers for added security.

For example, to configure MD5 authentication between BGP peers, you can use the following commands:

Copy code

neighbor 192.168.1.1 password mysecret neighbor 192.168.1.1 password encryption md5

These commands set a password and specify that MD5 encryption should be used for authentication.

Once BGP peers are configured and connected, they start exchanging BGP routing updates.

BGP uses the path attribute to determine the best path to a destination network.

The path attribute contains information about the route, including the AS numbers it has traversed.

To manipulate BGP routing decisions, administrators can configure BGP route maps using commands like:

pythonCopy code

route-map MYMAP permit 10 match as-path 1 set local-preference 200

This route map matches routes that have traversed AS path 1 and sets their local preference to 200, influencing BGP route selection.

Administrators often use BGP communities to tag routes with additional information.

For instance, to add a community tag to BGP routes, you can use commands like:

pythonCopy code

ip community-list 1 permit 65535:100 route-map SET-COMMUNITY permit 10 match community 1 set community 65535:200

In this example, routes matching community 1 are tagged with community 65535:200 using a route map.

BGP route filtering is essential to control which routes are advertised to BGP peers and which are not.

Administrators can use access control lists (ACLs) and prefix lists to filter BGP routes.

For instance, to filter BGP routes using a prefix list, you can configure:

sqlCopy code

```
ip prefix-list FILTER-PREFIXES seq 10 permit 192.168.0.0/16 router bgp 65535 neighbor 192.168.1.1 prefix-list FILTER-PREFIXES out
```

This configuration allows only routes matching the prefix 192.168.0.0/16 to be advertised to the BGP neighbor at IP address 192.168.1.1.

BGP route aggregation can be employed to reduce the size of the BGP table and improve routing efficiency.

To configure BGP route aggregation on a Cisco router, you can use commands like:

cssCopy code

```
router bgp 65535 aggregate-address 192.168.0.0 255.255.0.0 summary-only
```

This command aggregates routes within the 192.168.0.0/16 range into a single summary route.

Another essential aspect of BGP configuration is route dampening, a mechanism to suppress flapping routes that continuously go up and down.

To enable route dampening on a Cisco router, you can use commands like:

Copy code

```
router bgp 65535 bgp dampening
```

Route dampening helps stabilize the BGP routing table and reduce unnecessary route changes.

Additionally, BGP can be configured with route reflectors to address the scaling challenges associated with full-mesh BGP peerings.

Route reflectors help reduce the number of BGP peerings required in a large network.

To configure a route reflector on a Cisco router, you can use commands like:

Copy code

router bgp 65535 neighbor 192.168.1.1 route-reflector-client

This command designates the neighbor at IP address 192.168.1.1 as a route reflector client.

BGP communities can also be used in conjunction with route reflectors to control route propagation within the network.

Administrators can set and manipulate BGP communities to control how routes are propagated to route reflectors and their clients.

When configuring BGP route reflectors, it's crucial to ensure that the route reflector hierarchy is well-defined and that clients are appropriately configured.

Lastly, monitoring and regular maintenance of the BGP configuration are essential to ensure that the routing protocol continues to function optimally.

Administrators can use show commands to inspect BGP status, view BGP table information, and troubleshoot issues.

For example, to display BGP neighbor information on a Cisco router, you can use the command:

sqlCopy code

show bgp neighbors

This command provides details about BGP peerings, including their status and IP addresses.

In summary, BGP configuration is a complex and critical task for managing large-scale networks.

Understanding the fundamental concepts of AS numbers, BGP peers, route attributes, and best practices is essential.

Administrators can use CLI commands to configure BGP neighbors, authentication, route manipulation, route filtering, aggregation, and route reflectors.

Regular monitoring and maintenance are necessary to ensure the stability and reliability of BGP in a network environment.

Advanced routing policies are a crucial component of network management, allowing administrators to control and optimize the flow of traffic within a network.

To implement advanced routing policies effectively, administrators must understand the principles and techniques involved.

One essential concept in advanced routing policies is traffic engineering, which involves shaping and directing traffic flows to meet specific network objectives.

Traffic engineering can be achieved using various techniques, including route manipulation, quality of service (QoS), and policy-based routing.

To implement policy-based routing using Cisco routers, administrators can use the **route-map** and **ip policy** commands.

For example, to create a route map that matches traffic based on specific criteria, you can configure:

pythonCopy code

```
route-map POLICY-ROUTE permit 10 match ip address 101
set ip next-hop 192.168.1.1
```

This route map matches traffic specified in access list 101 and directs it to the next-hop IP address 192.168.1.1.

Quality of Service (QoS) is another critical aspect of advanced routing policies, allowing administrators to prioritize certain types of traffic over others.

To configure QoS on Cisco routers, you can use the **class-map**, **policy-map**, and **service-policy** commands.

For instance, to create a policy map that prioritizes VoIP traffic, you can set up:

pythonCopy code

```
class-map VOIP-TRAFFIC match access-group 100 policy-map QOS-POLICY class VOIP-TRAFFIC priority percent 30
```

This policy map matches traffic specified in access list 100 and assigns it a priority of 30% of available bandwidth.

Administrators can also use advanced routing policies to implement route redistribution between different routing protocols, such as OSPF and BGP.

Route redistribution allows networks with multiple routing protocols to exchange routing information.

To configure route redistribution on a Cisco router, you can use the **redistribute** command within the appropriate routing protocol configuration mode.

For example, to redistribute routes from OSPF into BGP, you can use commands like:

kotlinCopy code

```
router bgp 65535 redistribute ospf 1 match internal external 1 external 2 metric-type 1 metric 10000 100 255 1 1500
```

This command redistributes OSPF routes into BGP and specifies various parameters like metric values and filtering criteria.

Administrators should exercise caution when implementing route redistribution to avoid routing loops and unintended consequences.

Additionally, advanced routing policies often involve the use of access control lists (ACLs) to filter or modify traffic based on specific criteria, such as source or destination IP addresses.

For example, to create an ACL that matches traffic from a specific source IP address range, you can configure:

arduinoCopy code

```
access-list 101 permit ip 192.168.0.0 0.0.255.255 any
```

This ACL permits traffic from the 192.168.0.0/16 network to any destination.

Advanced routing policies are also used to implement traffic engineering techniques like load balancing and path optimization.

Load balancing distributes network traffic across multiple paths or links, ensuring efficient utilization and redundancy.

To configure load balancing on Cisco routers, administrators can use the **ip route** command with multiple next-hop IP addresses.

For instance, to enable load balancing between two equal-cost routes, you can use commands like:

Copy code

```
ip route 192.168.1.0 255.255.255.0 192.168.2.1 ip route
192.168.1.0 255.255.255.0 192.168.3.1
```

These commands specify two next-hop IP addresses for the same destination network, enabling load balancing.

Path optimization involves selecting the best path for traffic based on factors like latency, bandwidth, and network conditions.

To achieve path optimization, administrators can use routing protocols with built-in mechanisms like BGP's path selection algorithm.

BGP's path selection algorithm takes into account multiple attributes, such as AS path length and local preference, to determine the best path to a destination.

Administrators can influence this process by modifying BGP attributes using route maps and prefix lists.

Advanced routing policies also extend to the realm of security, where administrators use policies to enforce access control and protect against various threats.

For example, administrators can configure access control policies to filter traffic based on source and destination IP addresses and port numbers.

To implement an access control policy on a Cisco router, you can use the **access-list** and **access-group** commands.

For instance, to deny traffic from a specific source IP address range, you can configure:

arduinoCopy code

```
access-list 102 deny ip 192.168.0.0 0.0.255.255 any
```

This access control list denies traffic from the 192.168.0.0/16 network.

To apply this policy to an interface, you can use the **access-group** command:

kotlinCopy code

```
interface GigabitEthernet0/0 ip access-group 102 in
```

This command applies access list 102 to incoming traffic on interface GigabitEthernet0/0.

Advanced routing policies also encompass the use of route summarization and aggregation to reduce the size of routing tables and improve routing efficiency.

Route summarization combines multiple IP routes into a single summarized route, reducing the number of entries in routing tables.

To configure route summarization on a Cisco router, you can use the **ip summary-address** command within the routing protocol configuration mode.

For example, to summarize routes within the 192.168.0.0/16 range, you can use a command like:

cssCopy code

```
router ospf 1 summary-address 192.168.0.0 255.255.0.0
```

This command summarizes routes within the specified range for OSPF.

In summary, advanced routing policies encompass a wide range of techniques and configurations that enable administrators to shape, optimize, secure, and control network traffic effectively.

Understanding traffic engineering, QoS, route redistribution, ACLs, load balancing, path optimization, security policies, and route summarization is crucial for managing complex network environments.

Administrators can use CLI commands and configuration tools to implement these policies and tailor their networks to specific requirements and objectives.

## Chapter 4: VLAN Design and Implementation

VLAN (Virtual Local Area Network) trunking and inter-VLAN routing are essential networking techniques used to segment and manage traffic in modern network infrastructures.

VLAN trunking enables the transportation of multiple VLANs over a single physical link, allowing network administrators to efficiently utilize network resources.

To configure VLAN trunking on network switches, administrators can use CLI commands to define which VLANs should be allowed to traverse a specific trunk link.

For instance, on a Cisco switch, the **switchport trunk allowed vlan** command is used to specify the list of VLANs permitted on a trunk interface.

Administrators can issue a command like:

Copy code

switchport trunk allowed vlan 10,20,30

This command permits VLANs 10, 20, and 30 to traverse the trunk link.

Inter-VLAN routing, on the other hand, is the process of forwarding traffic between different VLANs.

To implement inter-VLAN routing, administrators can use a Layer 3 device, such as a router or Layer 3 switch, to route traffic between VLANs.

For example, to configure inter-VLAN routing on a Cisco router, administrators can create sub-interfaces on a router's Ethernet interface, each associated with a specific VLAN.

Using the **interface** command, they can define these sub-interfaces and assign them IP addresses corresponding to the respective VLANs.

A typical configuration might look like this:
kotlinCopy code

```
interface GigabitEthernet0/0.10 encapsulation dot1Q 10 ip
address       192.168.10.1      255.255.255.0      interface
GigabitEthernet0/0.20 encapsulation dot1Q 20 ip address
192.168.20.1 255.255.255.0
```

In this example, two sub-interfaces are created for VLANs 10 and 20, with their corresponding IP addresses.

The **encapsulation dot1Q** command specifies the VLAN tag associated with each sub-interface.

Additionally, a routing protocol or static routes can be configured on the router to facilitate traffic routing between the VLANs.

Inter-VLAN routing is crucial for ensuring communication between different segments of a network while maintaining logical isolation.

The combination of VLAN trunking and inter-VLAN routing allows network administrators to design and manage complex network architectures efficiently.

For larger networks, where scalability and performance are critical, Layer 3 switches are often used for inter-VLAN routing.

These switches have the capability to route traffic between VLANs directly at wire speed, reducing the need for external routers.

When implementing VLANs and inter-VLAN routing, careful consideration should be given to security and access control.

Access control lists (ACLs) can be used to filter traffic between VLANs, ensuring that only authorized traffic is allowed to cross VLAN boundaries.

For example, an ACL can be configured on a Layer 3 device to permit or deny traffic between specific VLANs or IP addresses.

To configure an ACL on a Cisco router for this purpose, administrators can use commands like:

arduinoCopy code

```
access-list 101 permit ip 192.168.10.0 0.0.0.255 any
access-list 101 deny ip any any
```

In this example, access list 101 permits traffic from VLAN 10 to any destination but denies all other traffic.

The access list can then be applied to the sub-interface to enforce the specified access control rules.

VLAN trunking and inter-VLAN routing are fundamental techniques used in various networking scenarios, such as in data centers, enterprise networks, and service provider networks.

They enable the creation of isolated broadcast domains, efficient resource utilization, and secure traffic segmentation.

Additionally, these techniques are crucial for ensuring that different parts of a network can communicate with each other while maintaining network security.

When configuring VLAN trunking and inter-VLAN routing, network administrators should follow best practices, document their configurations, and conduct thorough testing to ensure that traffic flows as expected.

Proper planning and implementation of VLANs and inter-VLAN routing contribute to a well-organized and secure network infrastructure that can adapt to changing business needs.


Q-in-Q tunneling, also known as IEEE 802.1ad or Provider Bridging, is a networking technique used to enhance scalability and flexibility in Ethernet networks.

This technique is particularly valuable in service provider networks and large enterprise environments where efficient management of VLANs and traffic isolation are essential.

Q-in-Q tunneling extends the capability of standard VLANs by allowing multiple layers of VLAN tags to be applied to Ethernet frames.

This means that instead of having a single VLAN tag in an Ethernet frame, you can have multiple nested VLAN tags, enabling a hierarchical approach to VLAN management.

The need for Q-in-Q tunneling arises when a network requires more than the 4,096 VLANs allowed by the standard 802.1Q VLAN tagging.

In such cases, service providers and large organizations may run out of available VLAN IDs, especially when serving multiple customers or departments.

By implementing Q-in-Q tunneling, you can effectively expand the VLAN space, as it allows for up to 4,094 additional VLANs within each standard VLAN.

To deploy Q-in-Q tunneling, network administrators need to configure the network devices, typically Ethernet switches and routers, to support this feature.

On Cisco switches, for example, you can enable Q-in-Q tunneling on an interface using the **dot1q tunnel** command:

kotlinCopy code

interface GigabitEthernet0/1 dot1q tunnel

This command enables Q-in-Q tunneling on GigabitEthernet0/1, allowing it to accept and process Ethernet frames with multiple VLAN tags.

When Q-in-Q is enabled on an interface, the device will add an additional VLAN tag (outer tag) to the incoming frames while preserving the original VLAN tag (inner tag).

The outer tag identifies the customer or service provider, while the inner tag identifies the VLAN within that customer's network.

This hierarchical tagging allows the service provider to maintain separation between customer VLANs and manage their network more efficiently.

One common use case for Q-in-Q tunneling is in Metro Ethernet networks, where service providers offer Ethernet services to multiple customers over a shared infrastructure.

Each customer's traffic is placed within a Q-in-Q tunnel, ensuring that it remains isolated from other customers' traffic and can use its VLAN numbering scheme.

Q-in-Q tunneling also simplifies network design, as it eliminates the need to assign unique VLAN IDs across different customer networks, making the deployment of Ethernet services more scalable.

Another benefit of Q-in-Q tunneling is that it reduces the complexity of configuration and troubleshooting, as each customer can maintain its VLAN IDs without concern for conflicts in the shared network.

To further illustrate this concept, imagine a service provider offering Ethernet services to multiple customers in a shared network.

Each customer has its set of VLANs and uses the same VLAN IDs across different sites.

With Q-in-Q tunneling, the service provider can assign a unique outer VLAN tag to each customer, ensuring that their traffic remains separate in the shared infrastructure.

This technique is particularly valuable when customers need to extend their Layer 2 networks across multiple locations while maintaining isolation and security.

In addition to enhancing scalability and traffic isolation, Q-in-Q tunneling can also improve network security by isolating traffic at multiple levels.

Administrators can implement access control and security policies based on both the inner and outer VLAN tags.

For example, a service provider can use the outer VLAN tag to control which customers can communicate with each other, while the inner VLAN tag allows customers to manage their own network traffic within their VLANs.

Q-in-Q tunneling is not limited to service provider networks; it can also be applied in large enterprise networks with complex VLAN requirements.

For instance, a large multinational corporation may have multiple subsidiaries, each with its own VLAN numbering scheme.

By implementing Q-in-Q tunneling, the parent company can assign an outer VLAN tag to each subsidiary, allowing them to maintain their VLAN IDs independently.

This approach simplifies network management and reduces the chances of VLAN ID conflicts.

In summary, Q-in-Q tunneling is a valuable networking technique that enhances scalability and flexibility by allowing nested VLAN tags in Ethernet frames.

It is particularly useful in service provider networks, where multiple customers or departments require separate VLANs and traffic isolation.

By enabling Q-in-Q tunneling on network devices, administrators can efficiently manage VLANs, extend Layer 2 networks, and simplify network design while maintaining security and isolation between different entities within the network.

## Chapter 5: Spanning Tree Protocol (STP) Optimization

Rapid Spanning Tree Protocol (RSTP) is an evolution of the original Spanning Tree Protocol (STP) designed to enhance network convergence and reduce the time it takes for a network to recover from topology changes.

STP was introduced to address the problem of loops in Ethernet networks, which can lead to broadcast storms and network instability.

STP works by electing a root bridge and creating a loop-free topology by blocking certain ports on network switches.

However, STP has limitations in terms of convergence time, as it can take several seconds for a network to reconverge after a topology change.

This delay can result in disruptions to network traffic, which is undesirable in modern networks that require high availability.

RSTP, also known as IEEE 802.1w, was developed to overcome these limitations by significantly reducing the convergence time.

One of the key features of RSTP is the rapid detection of topology changes.

In STP, the network convergence process involves multiple steps, including the listening and learning phases, which contribute to the delay.

RSTP streamlines this process by immediately transitioning ports to the forwarding state without waiting for the learning phase to complete.

This rapid transition minimizes the impact of topology changes on network traffic.

To deploy RSTP, network administrators need to enable it on compatible network switches.

Most modern Ethernet switches and routers support RSTP as part of their feature set.

For example, on a Cisco switch, administrators can enable RSTP using the following command:

Copy code

spanning-tree mode rapid-pvst

This command configures the switch to operate in RSTP mode with the Rapid PVST+ (Per VLAN Spanning Tree Plus) variation, which allows for separate RSTP instances per VLAN.

Once RSTP is enabled, the network devices start exchanging bridge protocol data units (BPDU) to establish the RSTP topology.

Another important aspect of RSTP is the use of the "Edge Port" concept.

In RSTP, certain ports can be configured as edge ports, which are ports that connect to end devices such as computers or printers.

Edge ports are considered safe and do not participate in the traditional STP or RSTP process, as they are not expected to cause loops in the network.

By designating edge ports, RSTP reduces the convergence time further by allowing these ports to immediately transition to the forwarding state.

To configure an edge port on a Cisco switch, administrators can use the following command:

Copy code

spanning-tree portfast

This command enables the PortFast feature on the selected interface, designating it as an edge port.

RSTP also introduces the concept of "Alternate" and "Backup" ports.

Alternate ports are designated as backup paths for redundant links and can transition to the forwarding state rapidly if the primary link fails.

Backup ports, on the other hand, are used to provide an alternate path in case the designated port (the one in forwarding state) fails.

These concepts help RSTP converge quickly in the presence of redundant links.

One of the significant advantages of RSTP is its backward compatibility with traditional STP.

When RSTP-capable switches are introduced into a network with existing STP switches, they can operate in a compatibility mode known as "STP mode."

This allows the RSTP switches to interoperate with the legacy STP switches while still benefiting from the rapid convergence capabilities of RSTP on their own links.

RSTP has become the default choice for Ethernet networks due to its rapid convergence and backward compatibility with STP.

It has largely replaced the older STP and the more advanced Multiple Spanning Tree Protocol (MSTP) in modern network deployments.

In summary, Rapid Spanning Tree Protocol (RSTP) is a crucial improvement over the original Spanning Tree Protocol (STP) for Ethernet networks.

RSTP offers rapid convergence in the event of topology changes, reducing network downtime and improving overall network performance.

To deploy RSTP, network administrators need to enable it on compatible switches and configure edge ports and other RSTP-specific features as needed.

By leveraging RSTP's capabilities, network professionals can build more resilient and responsive Ethernet networks that meet the demands of today's applications and services.

Multiple Spanning Tree Protocol (MSTP) is an advanced network protocol designed to provide efficient and flexible loop prevention and network redundancy solutions in complex Ethernet environments.

MSTP is an enhancement of the original Spanning Tree Protocol (STP) and the Rapid Spanning Tree Protocol (RSTP), offering improved scalability and customization.

MSTP allows network administrators to divide a network into multiple spanning tree instances, each serving a specific set of VLANs, which is particularly beneficial in large networks with numerous VLANs and different traffic requirements.

To configure MSTP on network devices, such as Cisco switches, administrators need to follow a series of steps that involve defining MST regions, configuring instances, and assigning VLANs to those instances.

MSTP operates by mapping multiple VLANs to a single spanning tree instance, which reduces the number of active spanning tree instances compared to STP or RSTP.

This consolidation of VLANs into instances simplifies network management while maintaining redundancy and loop prevention.

To enable MSTP on a Cisco switch, administrators can use the following CLI command:

Copy code

```
spanning-tree mode mst
```

This command sets the switch to operate in MSTP mode.

MSTP configuration begins with the definition of MST regions, which are logical groupings of switches that share the same MST configuration.

These regions help determine which switches will participate in a particular MST instance.

To configure an MST region on a Cisco switch, administrators can use the following commands:

Copy code

```
spanning-tree mst configuration name REGION_NAME
revision NUMBER
```

The **name** command assigns a name to the MST region, while the **revision** command specifies the MSTP revision number.

Each MST region should have a unique name and revision number to ensure correct operation.

Next, administrators need to define MST instances within the region.

An MST instance corresponds to a spanning tree topology that encompasses specific VLANs.

To create an MST instance, use the following CLI commands: goCopy code

```
spanning-tree mst configuration instance NUMBER vlan-
range VLAN_LIST
```

Here, **NUMBER** represents the instance number, while **VLAN_LIST** specifies the range of VLANs associated with that instance.

For example, to create an MST instance for VLANs 10 to 20, the command would be:
goCopy code

```
spanning-tree mst configuration instance 1 vlan-range 10-
20
```

After defining the MST region and instances, administrators must map VLANs to these instances.

This mapping dictates which VLANs belong to each instance and determines how MSTP calculates the spanning tree topology for each instance.

To map VLANs to an MST instance on a Cisco switch, use the following command:
Copy code

spanning-tree mst configuration instance NUMBER vlan VLAN_LIST

Here, **NUMBER** corresponds to the MST instance number, and **VLAN_LIST** specifies the list of VLANs associated with that instance.

For example, to map VLANs 10 and 20 to MST instance 1, the command would be:

Copy code

spanning-tree mst configuration instance 1 vlan 10,20

Once the VLAN-to-instance mappings are defined, MSTP will calculate the spanning tree topology for each MST instance based on the designated root bridge and designated ports for the mapped VLANs.

An essential aspect of MSTP is the concept of the Common Spanning Tree (CST).

The CST is a single spanning tree instance that encompasses all VLANs in the network and ensures loop prevention and redundancy for the entire network.

The CST operates alongside the MST instances and relies on their calculated topologies to determine the root bridge and designated ports for the shared VLANs.

MSTP provides a way to configure the CST by specifying a priority for the CST instance within the MST region.

To set the CST priority on a Cisco switch, use the following command:

Copy code

spanning-tree mst configuration instance 0 priority PRIORITY

Here, **PRIORITY** represents the priority value for the CST instance.

A lower priority value results in the switch being selected as the CST root bridge for the MST region.

In addition to configuring MSTP, administrators can monitor and verify the status of MST instances and CST by using various CLI commands.

For instance, to display information about the MSTP configuration and MST instances on a Cisco switch, use the following command:

sqlCopy code

show spanning-tree mst

This command provides details about the MST region, instance, VLAN mapping, and CST configuration.

In summary, Multiple Spanning Tree Protocol (MSTP) is a powerful tool for managing network redundancy and loop prevention in complex Ethernet environments with multiple VLANs.

By dividing the network into MST regions, configuring instances, and mapping VLANs to those instances, network administrators can customize MSTP to meet the specific requirements of their network.

MSTP provides a way to simplify network management while ensuring high availability and redundancy.

Using CLI commands like those mentioned earlier, administrators can configure, monitor, and maintain MSTP configurations on their network switches, providing a reliable and efficient networking solution for modern environments.

## Chapter 6: Campus LAN Security Strategies

Port security and VLAN hopping prevention are critical security measures that network administrators can implement to protect their networks from unauthorized access and security threats.

Port security is a feature found in many Ethernet switches that enables administrators to control which devices are allowed to connect to specific switch ports.

It works by associating a specific MAC address or a limited number of MAC addresses with a switch port and blocking all other MAC addresses from accessing that port.

Port security is commonly used to prevent unauthorized devices from gaining network access.

To configure port security on a Cisco switch, you can use the following CLI command:

Copy code

```
switchport port-security
```

This command enables port security on the selected switch port.

Once enabled, administrators can specify various parameters, including the maximum number of allowed MAC addresses and the action to take when a violation occurs.

For example, to allow only one MAC address on a port and disable the port if a violation occurs, you can use the following commands:

arduinoCopy code

```
switchport port-security maximum 1 switchport port-security violation shutdown
```

With these settings, the switch will only allow one MAC address to communicate through the port, and if any other MAC address is detected, the port will be shut down.

Port security provides an effective way to control network access and protect against unauthorized devices connecting to the network.

VLAN hopping, on the other hand, is a security vulnerability that can occur in situations where a switch port is not properly configured to prevent it.

VLAN hopping occurs when an attacker on one VLAN gains unauthorized access to traffic on another VLAN.

This can be particularly problematic in multi-tenant environments where multiple VLANs share the same physical infrastructure.

One common method of VLAN hopping is known as double tagging, where an attacker sends frames with multiple VLAN tags in an attempt to trick the switch into forwarding the frames to an unintended VLAN.

To prevent VLAN hopping, administrators should implement techniques such as VLAN access control lists (VACLs) and protected ports.

VACLs allow administrators to define rules that restrict traffic between VLANs, preventing unauthorized communication.

To configure VACLs on a Cisco switch, you can use the following CLI command:

pythonCopy code

```
vlan access-map NAME 10 match ip address ACL_NUMBER
action drop
```

This command creates an access map and associates it with a VLAN, specifying which traffic should be dropped based on an access control list (ACL).

Protected ports, also known as private VLAN edge (PVLAN Edge) ports, are another technique to prevent VLAN hopping.

Protected ports are isolated from each other and do not forward traffic to other protected ports on the same switch.

To enable protected ports on a Cisco switch, you can use the following CLI command:

arduinoCopy code

```
switchport protected
```

This command configures the selected port as a protected port.

Both VACLs and protected ports are effective measures to prevent VLAN hopping and maintain the security and isolation of VLANs.

In addition to port security and VLAN hopping prevention, network administrators should also consider implementing other security measures, such as 802.1X authentication and network segmentation.

802.1X authentication is a port-based access control protocol that requires users or devices to authenticate before gaining network access.

It can be used to ensure that only authorized devices can connect to the network.

To configure 802.1X authentication on a Cisco switch, administrators can use the following CLI command:

arduinoCopy code

```
dot1x port-control auto
```

This command enables 802.1X authentication on the selected port and sets it to automatically control port access based on authentication results.

Network segmentation involves dividing a network into smaller, isolated segments or VLANs, each with its own security policies.

Segmentation helps contain security breaches and limit the impact of security incidents.

By segmenting the network and applying security policies to each segment, administrators can improve network security.

In summary, port security and VLAN hopping prevention are essential security measures for protecting Ethernet networks from unauthorized access and security threats.

Port security controls which devices can connect to switch ports, while VLAN hopping prevention techniques like VACLs and protected ports safeguard against attacks that attempt to compromise VLAN isolation.

When combined with other security measures like 802.1X authentication and network segmentation, these techniques contribute to a comprehensive network security strategy that helps organizations defend against evolving threats and maintain the integrity of their networks.

Intrusion detection and prevention in the LAN is a crucial aspect of network security, aimed at safeguarding the integrity and confidentiality of data within the local area network.

LANs, or Local Area Networks, are often the foundation of an organization's communication infrastructure, connecting computers, servers, and other devices to facilitate data exchange and collaboration.

However, with the increasing sophistication of cyber threats, LANs are susceptible to various forms of intrusions, including unauthorized access, malware, and network attacks.

To address these security challenges, network administrators implement Intrusion Detection Systems (IDS) and Intrusion Prevention Systems (IPS) within the LAN.

An IDS is a network security tool designed to monitor network traffic and identify suspicious or malicious activities.

It operates by analyzing network packets, looking for patterns or behaviors that match known attack signatures or anomalies that deviate from normal network traffic.

One widely used open-source IDS is Snort, which can be configured using a set of rules to detect and alert on specific network activities.

For example, administrators can create rules to detect port scanning attempts or unusual traffic patterns within the LAN.

To configure Snort rules for detecting suspicious activities, administrators can use the following CLI command:

cssCopy code

```
sudo snort -q -c /etc/snort/snort.conf -A fast -q -y -v -o -l /var/log/snort
```

This command starts Snort with specific options and configuration files, enabling it to analyze network traffic according to predefined rules.

While IDS systems are valuable for identifying potential threats within the LAN, Intrusion Prevention Systems (IPS) take security a step further by actively blocking or mitigating detected threats.

An IPS can be thought of as an advanced firewall that not only detects malicious activities but also takes action to prevent them from harming the network.

Cisco's Intrusion Prevention System (IPS) is a widely used commercial solution that offers real-time threat prevention for LANs.

To configure Cisco IPS to protect a LAN, administrators can use the following CLI command:

kotlinCopy code

```
configure terminal interface vlan VLAN_NUMBER ip ips MY_IPS_POLICY in
```

This command configures the IPS policy on a specific VLAN interface, allowing the IPS to inspect traffic on that VLAN and take actions based on the defined policy.

Intrusion detection and prevention in the LAN can also benefit from the integration of Security Information and Event Management (SIEM) systems.

SIEM solutions aggregate and analyze security event data from various sources, including IDS and IPS, to provide a comprehensive view of network security.

One popular open-source SIEM solution is ELK Stack, which combines Elasticsearch, Logstash, and Kibana to collect, process, and visualize security data.

To deploy ELK Stack for LAN intrusion detection and prevention, administrators can use the following CLI commands for installation and setup:

arduinoCopy code

```
sudo apt-get install elasticsearch logstash kibana
```

These commands install the ELK Stack components on a Linux server, which can then be configured to collect and analyze security data from IDS and IPS systems.

Intrusion detection and prevention in the LAN are not only about technical solutions but also about security policies and practices.

Network administrators should establish clear security policies that define acceptable use, access controls, and incident response procedures.

User education and awareness programs can also play a crucial role in preventing security breaches, as employees are often the first line of defense against social engineering attacks and phishing attempts.

Regular monitoring and auditing of LAN traffic, along with the timely application of security patches and updates, are essential for maintaining the security of the LAN.

Additionally, implementing strong authentication mechanisms such as multi-factor authentication (MFA) can further enhance LAN security by ensuring that only authorized users gain access to the network.

In summary, intrusion detection and prevention in the LAN are vital components of network security, designed to protect the integrity and confidentiality of data within the local area network.

Through the use of Intrusion Detection Systems (IDS), Intrusion Prevention Systems (IPS), Security Information and Event Management (SIEM) solutions, and robust security policies and practices, organizations can defend against a wide range of cyber threats that target their LAN infrastructure.

By actively monitoring and responding to security incidents, LAN administrators can help safeguard their networks and protect sensitive information from unauthorized access and malicious activities.

# Chapter 7: Multilayer Switching and High Availability

High Availability and Network Redundancy are critical components of modern networks, ensuring uninterrupted service delivery and minimizing downtime in case of failures. Several protocols and technologies are available to achieve network redundancy, including HSRP (Hot Standby Router Protocol), VRRP (Virtual Router Redundancy Protocol), and GLBP (Gateway Load Balancing Protocol).

These protocols are designed to provide fault tolerance, load balancing, and failover capabilities in LAN environments.

HSRP is a Cisco proprietary protocol that allows multiple routers to work together to provide a virtual gateway IP address to the LAN hosts.

By designating one router as the active router and another as the standby router, HSRP ensures that there is always a backup router ready to take over if the active router fails.

To configure HSRP on Cisco routers, administrators can use the following CLI commands:

graphqlCopy code

```
interface INTERFACE standby GROUP_IP IP_ADDRESS
standby GROUP_IP IP_ADDRESS secondary standby
GROUP_IP IP_ADDRESS track INTERFACE standby
GROUP_IP IP_ADDRESS preempt
```

These commands configure HSRP on a router interface, specifying the virtual IP address, secondary IP address, interface tracking, and preemptive capabilities.

VRRP is an industry-standard protocol similar to HSRP but without vendor-specific limitations.

VRRP enables multiple routers to collaborate to provide a virtual IP address as the default gateway for LAN hosts.

Like HSRP, VRRP designates one router as the master router and others as backup routers.

VRRP routers exchange advertisement packets to determine the master router, ensuring a smooth failover process.

To configure VRRP on Cisco routers, administrators can use the following CLI commands:

graphqlCopy code

```
interface INTERFACE vrrp GROUP_IP IP_ADDRESS vrrp GROUP_IP IP_ADDRESS secondary vrrp GROUP_IP IP_ADDRESS track INTERFACE vrrp GROUP_IP priority PRIORITY vrrp GROUP_IP preempt
```

These commands configure VRRP on a router interface, specifying the virtual IP address, secondary IP address, interface tracking, priority, and preemptive capabilities.

GLBP, on the other hand, is also a Cisco proprietary protocol but offers more advanced load balancing capabilities compared to HSRP and VRRP.

GLBP allows multiple routers to share the load of serving as the default gateway for LAN hosts.

Unlike HSRP and VRRP, where one router is active and the others are standby, in GLBP, all routers can actively participate in forwarding traffic, distributing the load among them.

GLBP routers elect an AVG (Active Virtual Gateway) that assigns virtual MAC addresses to LAN hosts, ensuring that traffic is distributed efficiently.

To configure GLBP on Cisco routers, administrators can use the following CLI commands:

graphqlCopy code

```
interface INTERFACE glbp GROUP_IP IP_ADDRESS glbp GROUP_IP load-balancing weighted glbp GROUP_IP priority PRIORITY
```

These commands configure GLBP on a router interface, specifying the virtual IP address, load-balancing method, priority, and other parameters.

When deploying these redundancy protocols, administrators should consider factors such as network topology, router capabilities, and redundancy goals.

HSRP, VRRP, and GLBP can coexist in the same network, offering different levels of redundancy for various LAN segments.

It's essential to design the network with failover scenarios in mind, ensuring that all critical services have redundant paths and that failover times meet the organization's requirements.

Monitoring and regular testing of the redundancy configurations are also crucial to ensure that the failover mechanisms work as expected.

Additionally, administrators should document their configurations thoroughly and maintain up-to-date records of the active and standby routers for each redundancy group.

This documentation can be invaluable during troubleshooting and when planning for network upgrades or changes.

In summary, HSRP, VRRP, and GLBP are essential protocols for achieving network redundancy and high availability in LAN environments.

Each protocol has its advantages and use cases, making them valuable tools for ensuring uninterrupted network services and minimizing downtime in case of router or link failures.

By carefully configuring and managing these protocols, network administrators can create robust and reliable networks that meet the demands of today's connected world.

EtherChannel and Link Aggregation are networking techniques that provide enhanced bandwidth, fault tolerance, and load balancing by combining multiple physical links into a single logical link.

These techniques are particularly valuable in scenarios where high availability and increased throughput are essential, such as data centers and enterprise networks.

EtherChannel is Cisco's proprietary implementation of Link Aggregation, while Link Aggregation is a standard IEEE 802.3ad technology used by various networking vendors.

Both EtherChannel and Link Aggregation aim to bundle multiple physical links, or ports, into a single logical channel, resulting in higher aggregate bandwidth and improved network resilience.

To configure EtherChannel on Cisco devices, administrators can use the following CLI commands:

goCopy code

```
interface range GigabitEthernet0/1 - 4 channel-group 1 mode desirable
```

These commands create an EtherChannel group and assign the specified ports to it, setting the negotiation mode to "desirable" for dynamic negotiation with the connected switch.

On the other hand, configuring Link Aggregation (LACP) on non-Cisco devices involves using different CLI commands:

vbnetCopy code

```
interface range gigabitethernet 1/0/1 to 1/0/4 channel-group 1 mode active
```

In this example, the ports are assigned to a Link Aggregation group, and the mode is set to "active" for LACP negotiation.

The main difference between EtherChannel and Link Aggregation is the protocol used for negotiation.

EtherChannel uses Cisco's proprietary PAgP (Port Aggregation Protocol), while Link Aggregation uses IEEE 802.3ad's LACP (Link Aggregation Control Protocol).

Both protocols achieve the same goal of dynamically forming link aggregations based on the configuration and capabilities of the connected switches.

Once configured, EtherChannel or Link Aggregation provides several benefits:

**Increased Bandwidth**: By bundling multiple physical links, the logical channel enjoys higher combined bandwidth, allowing for faster data transfer.

**Load Balancing**: Traffic is distributed across the member links, preventing network congestion and optimizing resource utilization.

**Redundancy**: In the event of a link or switch failure, traffic is automatically rerouted through the remaining active links, ensuring network availability.

**Simplified Management**: Instead of managing individual links, administrators deal with a single logical interface, simplifying configuration and troubleshooting.

It's important to note that for EtherChannel and Link Aggregation to work correctly, both ends of the connection (switches or routers) must support the same negotiation protocol (PAgP or LACP) and configuration.

Additionally, the physical links within the bundle should have similar characteristics, such as speed and duplex settings, to avoid compatibility issues.

In terms of deployment scenarios, EtherChannel or Link Aggregation is commonly used to connect switches, routers, or servers to provide redundancy and load balancing.

For example, in a data center environment, multiple connections from a server to a switch can be aggregated into an EtherChannel or Link Aggregation group to ensure high availability and maximize throughput.

In practice, the specific configuration and deployment of EtherChannel or Link Aggregation depend on the network's requirements and the equipment in use.

In summary, EtherChannel and Link Aggregation are essential techniques for achieving increased network bandwidth, load balancing, and fault tolerance by combining multiple physical links into a single logical link.

While EtherChannel is Cisco's proprietary implementation, Link Aggregation follows the IEEE 802.3ad standard and is used by various networking vendors.

Both techniques offer benefits such as increased bandwidth, load balancing, redundancy, and simplified management, making them valuable tools for modern network deployments.

Administrators should carefully plan and configure these techniques to ensure compatibility and optimal performance in their specific network environments.

## Chapter 8: IPv6 Implementation and Transition

IPv6, the successor to IPv4, is a critical part of the modern internet's infrastructure, designed to address the exhaustion of IPv4 addresses and provide improved functionality for a growing number of connected devices.

IPv6 introduces several significant changes, most notably in addressing and configuration, to accommodate the exponential growth of the internet and overcome the limitations of its predecessor, IPv4.

One of the most noticeable differences between IPv6 and IPv4 is the format of the IP addresses themselves.

IPv4 uses a 32-bit address format, resulting in roughly 4.3 billion unique addresses, which have been nearly exhausted due to the rapid proliferation of devices connected to the internet.

In contrast, IPv6 uses a 128-bit address format, which allows for an astronomical number of unique addresses— approximately 340 undecillion (3.4 x 10^38) addresses.

The increased address space of IPv6 not only solves the address exhaustion problem but also introduces several improvements in address allocation and management.

IPv6 addresses consist of eight groups of four hexadecimal digits separated by colons, such as "2001:0db8:85a3:0000:0000:8a2e:0370:7334."

To simplify IPv6 address representation, consecutive groups of zeros within an address can be replaced with a double colon "::."

For example, the address "2001:0db8:85a3:0000:0000:8a2e:0370:7334" can be abbreviated as "2001:db8:85a3::8a2e:370:7334."

One of the key deployment considerations when configuring IPv6 is the allocation and assignment of IP addresses.

IPv6 addresses are typically assigned using one of the following methods: Stateless Address Autoconfiguration (SLAAC) and Dynamic Host Configuration Protocol version 6 (DHCPv6).

SLAAC is a stateless mechanism that allows devices to automatically configure their IPv6 addresses without relying on a central DHCP server.

In a SLAAC-enabled network, routers periodically broadcast Router Advertisement (RA) messages containing information about the network's IPv6 prefix and other configuration details.

Devices on the network listen for these RA messages and use the information to create their own IPv6 addresses.

For example, a device might receive an RA message with the prefix "2001:db8:85a3::/64" and generate its IPv6 address by appending a unique interface identifier.

The resulting address might be "2001:db8:85a3:0:abcd:effe:1234:5678."

On the other hand, DHCPv6 is a stateful method of IP address assignment that involves a DHCPv6 server, which can provide not only IP addresses but also additional configuration parameters, such as DNS server addresses and network settings.

To configure IPv6 addressing using DHCPv6, network administrators can set up a DHCPv6 server and configure the DHCPv6 clients to request addresses and other information.

For example, on a Cisco router, administrators can use the following CLI commands to configure DHCPv6:

yamlCopy code

```
ipv6 dhcp pool DHCP_POOL_NAME address prefix 2001:db8:85a3::/64 lifetime 1800 600 dns-server 2001:4860:4860::8888
```

These commands create a DHCPv6 pool, specify the IPv6 prefix to be assigned, set lease lifetimes, and define the DNS server address to be provided to clients.

Another crucial aspect of IPv6 configuration is router advertisements.

RA messages are critical for IPv6 autoconfiguration because they inform devices about the network's characteristics and provide prefixes for address generation.

Network administrators can configure RA messages on routers using CLI commands.

For example, to enable RA messages on a Cisco router interface, the following command can be used:

rubyCopy code

interface GigabitEthernet0/0 ipv6 address 2001:db8:85a3::1/64 ipv6 nd prefix 2001:db8:85a3::/64

These commands assign an IPv6 address to the router's interface and configure it to advertise the specified prefix to connected devices.

In addition to SLAAC and DHCPv6, IPv6 supports privacy extensions, which allow devices to periodically change their interface identifiers to enhance privacy and security.

This feature is particularly useful in preventing tracking of devices based on their IPv6 addresses.

In summary, IPv6 addressing and configuration bring significant changes to the way devices obtain and manage IP addresses compared to IPv4.

The expanded address space, the introduction of SLAAC and DHCPv6 for address assignment, and privacy extensions for enhanced security are all critical components of IPv6 deployment.

Understanding how to configure IPv6 addressing using these methods and manage RA messages is essential for network administrators looking to harness the full potential of IPv6 in their networks.

As the adoption of IPv6 continues to grow, it's important for network professionals to become proficient in IPv6 addressing and configuration to support the ever-expanding number of connected devices and ensure the longevity and scalability of their networks.

IPv6 Transition Mechanisms play a crucial role in enabling the seamless coexistence of IPv6 and IPv4 networks during the transition from the old IPv4 protocol to the new IPv6 protocol. These mechanisms are essential because the transition to IPv6 is not an instantaneous process; it's a gradual migration that requires compatibility and interoperability between the two protocols.

One of the key challenges during the transition is that the IPv4 and IPv6 address spaces are inherently different. IPv4 uses 32-bit addresses, while IPv6 uses 128-bit addresses. This difference in address length makes it challenging for IPv6-only devices to communicate with IPv4-only devices.

To address this challenge, various IPv6 Transition Mechanisms have been developed, and each has its specific use cases and deployment scenarios.

One of the most common IPv6 Transition Mechanisms is Dual Stack. In a Dual Stack configuration, devices and routers are configured to support both IPv4 and IPv6 simultaneously. This allows devices to communicate with each other using either IPv4 or IPv6, depending on the availability of compatible addresses.

To configure Dual Stack on a router, administrators can use CLI commands to assign both IPv4 and IPv6 addresses to the router's interfaces. For example:

cssCopy code

interface GigabitEthernet0/0 ip address 192.168.1.1
255.255.255.0 ipv6 address 2001:db8::1/64

These commands configure both an IPv4 address
(192.168.1.1) and an IPv6 address (2001:db8::1) on the
router's interface.

Another commonly used IPv6 Transition Mechanism is
Tunneling. Tunneling allows IPv6 packets to be encapsulated
within IPv4 packets, effectively creating a tunnel through an
IPv4 network. This enables IPv6 traffic to traverse IPv4-only
segments of the network.

One widely used tunneling protocol is 6in4, which
encapsulates IPv6 packets within IPv4 packets and is often
used to create IPv6-over-IPv4 tunnels between routers.

To configure a 6in4 tunnel on a router, administrators can
use CLI commands like the following:

cssCopy code

interface Tunnel0 description IPv6 Tunnel to Remote Site
tunnel source 203.0.113.1 tunnel destination 203.0.113.2
ipv6 address 2001:db8:1::1/64 tunnel mode ipv6ip 6to4

In this example, a tunnel interface (Tunnel0) is created, and
IPv6 traffic is encapsulated within IPv4 packets using the
6to4 tunneling mode. The tunnel source and destination
IPv4 addresses are specified, along with an IPv6 address for
the tunnel interface.

Another important IPv6 Transition Mechanism is Network
Address Translation for IPv6 (NAT66). NAT66 allows multiple
devices within a private IPv6 network to share a single public
IPv6 address when communicating with external IPv6
networks. This is similar to the NAT44 mechanism used in
IPv4.

To configure NAT66 on a router, administrators can use CLI
commands like the following:

typescriptCopy code

```
ipv6 access-list ACL_NAME permit ipv6 any any ipv6 nat
NAT66_NAME source list ACL_NAME pool POOL_NAME
interface GigabitEthernet0/0 ipv6 nat NAT66_NAME in
```

In this example, an IPv6 access control list (ACL) is created to permit traffic, and a NAT66 rule is defined to translate source IPv6 addresses from the internal network using a NAT pool. The NAT66 rule is applied to the router's interface.

These IPv6 Transition Mechanisms—Dual Stack, Tunneling, and NAT66—play a pivotal role in enabling the coexistence and transition between IPv4 and IPv6 networks.

Another important mechanism is the IPv6-over-IPv4 tunneling technique called 6to4. 6to4 allows IPv6 packets to be encapsulated within IPv4 packets, allowing for IPv6 communication over an IPv4 infrastructure.

To configure a 6to4 tunnel, a device typically needs a public IPv4 address. The following CLI commands demonstrate how to configure a 6to4 tunnel on a router:

cssCopy code

```
interface Tunnel0 description 6to4 Tunnel to IPv6 Network
no ip address ipv6 address 2002:IPv4PREFIX::1/16 tunnel
source GigabitEthernet0/0 tunnel mode ipv6ip 6to4
```

In this example, a tunnel interface (Tunnel0) is created, and an IPv6 address is assigned to it using the 6to4 prefix derived from the router's IPv4 address. The tunnel source is set to the router's IPv4 interface, enabling the encapsulation of IPv6 packets within IPv4 packets.

Additionally, there is the Intra-Site Automatic Tunnel Addressing Protocol (ISATAP), which allows IPv6 communication within an IPv4 intranet.

To configure ISATAP on a Windows computer, administrators can use the following CLI commands:

kotlinCopy code

netsh interface ipv6 isatap set state enabled netsh interface ipv6 isatap set router 192.168.1.1

These commands enable ISATAP on the computer and specify the IPv4 address of the ISATAP router.

Overall, IPv6 Transition Mechanisms are essential for a smooth migration from IPv4 to IPv6. Dual Stack, Tunneling (including 6in4, 6to4, and ISATAP), and NAT66 are key techniques used to ensure interoperability and compatibility between the two protocols.

By understanding and deploying these mechanisms effectively, network administrators can facilitate the coexistence of IPv4 and IPv6 networks, enabling a gradual transition to the new IPv6 protocol while maintaining connectivity with existing IPv4 infrastructure.

In summary, IPv6 Transition Mechanisms are vital tools for network administrators as they navigate the transition from IPv4 to IPv6.

These mechanisms, such as Dual Stack, Tunneling, and NAT66, provide the flexibility and compatibility needed to ensure a smooth migration while preserving connectivity and functionality across both IPv4 and IPv6 networks.

By mastering the deployment of these mechanisms through CLI commands and understanding their specific use cases, network professionals can successfully manage the coexistence and transition between IPv4 and IPv6 in their networks, paving the way for a more robust and scalable internet infrastructure.

## Chapter 9: Network Design for Large Campuses

Designing a Core and Distribution Layer in a network infrastructure is a critical aspect of creating a robust and efficient network architecture. These layers are fundamental building blocks that play a pivotal role in ensuring high-performance, scalability, and reliability of the network.

The Core Layer serves as the backbone of the network, responsible for fast and efficient data forwarding between different parts of the network. Its primary function is to provide high-speed connectivity and minimize latency. To design an effective Core Layer, network administrators need to consider factors such as redundancy, fault tolerance, and high availability.

One approach to achieving redundancy and fault tolerance in the Core Layer is to deploy multiple core routers or switches and use a protocol like the Hot Standby Router Protocol (HSRP) or Virtual Router Redundancy Protocol (VRRP) to ensure seamless failover in case of a core device failure.

For instance, to configure HSRP on a pair of routers, the following CLI commands can be used:

kotlinCopy code

interface GigabitEthernet0/0 ip address 192.168.1.1 255.255.255.0 standby 1 ip 192.168.1.254 standby 1 priority 110 standby 1 preempt

In this example, the router has two GigabitEthernet interfaces with HSRP enabled. The **standby** commands configure the virtual IP address (VIP) and the priority of the router in the HSRP group.

While the Core Layer focuses on high-speed connectivity, the Distribution Layer serves as an intermediary between the Core Layer and the Access Layer. It plays a crucial role in traffic distribution, access control, and segmentation. To design an effective Distribution Layer, administrators need to consider factors like access policies, VLAN segmentation, and routing between different subnets.

Using the Border Gateway Protocol (BGP) at the Distribution Layer can enhance network stability and redundancy by providing dynamic routing and traffic load balancing between multiple Internet Service Providers (ISPs).

To configure BGP on a distribution router, the following CLI commands can be used:

csharpCopy code

```
router bgp 65001 neighbor 203.0.113.1 remote- as 65002
neighbor 203.0.113.1 description ISP1 network 192.0.2.0
mask 255.255.255.0
```

In this example, BGP is configured with a local AS number of 65001. The **neighbor** command establishes a BGP peering session with the ISP's router at IP address 203.0.113.1. The **network** command advertises the local network to the ISP.

Segmentation of VLANs in the Distribution Layer is another crucial consideration. By implementing Virtual LANs (VLANs) and configuring inter-VLAN routing, administrators can control traffic flow and enforce security policies.

To configure VLANs and inter-VLAN routing on a distribution switch, the following CLI commands can be used:

kotlinCopy code

```
vlan 10 name Sales ! vlan 20 name Marketing ! interface
GigabitEthernet0/1 switchport mode trunk switchport trunk
allowed vlan 10,20 ! interface Vlan10 ip address
```

192.168.10.1 255.255.255.0 ! interface Vlan20 ip address 192.168.20.1 255.255.255.0

In this example, VLANs 10 and 20 are created with associated names. The **interface** commands configure a trunk port for VLAN traffic, and the VLAN interfaces are assigned IP addresses for routing purposes.

Security is another critical aspect of designing the Distribution Layer. Access control lists (ACLs) can be applied to filter traffic and enforce security policies. For instance, to deny traffic from a specific IP address range, the following CLI commands can be used:

sqlCopy code

```
access-list 101 deny ip 192.168.30.0 0.0.0.255 any
access-list 101 permit ip any any ! interface GigabitEthernet0/2 ip access-group 101 in
```

In this example, ACL 101 is configured to deny traffic from the 192.168.30.0/24 network and permit all other traffic. The ACL is then applied to an interface to filter incoming traffic.

In summary, designing an effective Core and Distribution Layer involves careful consideration of redundancy, fault tolerance, high availability, traffic distribution, access control, segmentation, and security. Using CLI commands and protocols like HSRP, VRRP, BGP, VLANs, and ACLs, network administrators can create a network architecture that meets the demands of modern businesses and ensures reliable and efficient connectivity. A well-designed Core and Distribution Layer forms the foundation of a scalable and resilient network infrastructure.

WAN Connectivity and Remote Site Integration are essential components of modern network design, allowing organizations to connect geographically dispersed locations and enable seamless communication and data sharing across their entire network infrastructure.

One common method for establishing WAN connectivity is through the use of leased lines, which provide a dedicated and reliable connection between remote sites and the central data center. To deploy a leased line, organizations typically need to work with a service provider to provision the circuit and configure the appropriate networking equipment.

In many cases, WAN connectivity is achieved using technologies like Frame Relay, MPLS (Multiprotocol Label Switching), or more recently, SD-WAN (Software-Defined Wide Area Network). SD-WAN, in particular, has gained popularity due to its flexibility and cost-effectiveness. It allows organizations to use multiple Internet connections, including broadband and 4G/5G, to create a highly available and resilient WAN. Configuration of SD-WAN devices involves defining policies and rules to determine how traffic is routed over different links.

For instance, to configure an SD-WAN device to prioritize VoIP traffic over other types of data, network administrators might use CLI commands like:

kotlinCopy code

policy-map QoS class voip priority class class-default fair-queue ! interface GigabitEthernet0/0 bandwidth 10000 service-policy output QoS !

In this example, a Quality of Service (QoS) policy is defined to prioritize VoIP traffic, ensuring low latency and high quality for voice calls.

Remote Site Integration often involves deploying routers or SD-WAN devices at remote locations to establish secure and efficient connections with the central data center. These devices need to be properly configured to establish VPN

(Virtual Private Network) tunnels or secure communication channels.

For instance, to configure a VPN tunnel between two remote sites, administrators might use CLI commands like:

pythonCopy code

```
crypto isakmp policy 10 encr aes authentication pre-share group 2 ! crypto isakmp key secretpassword address 203.0.113.1 ! crypto ipsec transform-set myset esp-aes esp-sha-hmac ! crypto map mymap 10 ipsec-isakmp set peer 203.0.113.1 set transform-set myset match address 100 ! access-list 100 permit ip 192.168.10.0 0.0.0.255 192.168.20.0 0.0.0.255 !
```

In this example, a VPN tunnel is established between two remote sites using IPsec encryption. The configuration includes specifying encryption and authentication settings, defining a transform-set, and creating an access list to determine which traffic is allowed through the tunnel.

Security is a paramount concern when integrating remote sites into a WAN. It's crucial to implement proper access control measures, firewall rules, and intrusion detection systems to protect the network from external threats. Network administrators must regularly update security policies and deploy security patches to ensure the network remains resilient to emerging threats.

To enhance security, organizations may also use technologies like Virtual Private Networks (VPNs) for remote site connectivity. VPNs provide encrypted and secure communication channels over public networks like the Internet. They can be configured using CLI commands or dedicated VPN appliances, depending on the organization's requirements.

Another critical aspect of WAN connectivity and remote site integration is monitoring and management. Network administrators need to have visibility into the performance and health of the WAN links and remote devices. SNMP (Simple Network Management Protocol) can be used to collect data from network devices and monitor their status.

For instance, to enable SNMP on a router, administrators might use CLI commands like:

Copy code

```
snmp-server community mycommunity RO snmp-server
host 203.0.113.2 mycommunity
```

In this example, SNMP is configured with a community string "mycommunity" and a monitoring host at IP address 203.0.113.2.

Additionally, organizations may deploy Network Performance Monitoring (NPM) and Network Traffic Analysis (NTA) tools to gain deeper insights into network traffic patterns and identify performance bottlenecks.

In summary, WAN Connectivity and Remote Site Integration are integral components of modern network design. Organizations can deploy various technologies, such as leased lines, MPLS, SD-WAN, and VPNs, to establish connectivity between remote sites and the central data center. Configuration of these technologies often involves the use of CLI commands to define policies, security settings, and routing rules. Security, monitoring, and management play a vital role in ensuring the reliability and performance of the WAN infrastructure. By carefully planning and configuring WAN connectivity, organizations can create a robust and efficient network that meets their business needs.

Traffic Engineering and Load Balancing are critical aspects of network management that focus on optimizing the flow of data across a network, ensuring efficient resource utilization, and improving overall network performance.

In modern network environments, it is common for networks to carry a diverse range of traffic types, including voice, video, data, and various applications. To manage this traffic effectively, network administrators often deploy traffic engineering techniques to allocate network resources efficiently and maintain the desired Quality of Service (QoS).

One of the fundamental tools used for traffic engineering is Quality of Service (QoS). QoS allows network administrators to classify and prioritize network traffic, ensuring that critical applications receive the necessary bandwidth and latency requirements. CLI commands can be employed to configure QoS policies on network devices.

For instance, to configure QoS on a router, administrators might use CLI commands like:

```python
pythonCopy code
class-map match-all voice match access-group 101 !
policy-map QoS class voice priority percent 30 class
class-default fair-queue ! interface GigabitEthernet0/0
service-policy output QoS ! access-list 101 permit udp any
any range 16384 32767
```

In this example, a QoS policy is defined to prioritize voice traffic (e.g., VoIP) by allocating 30% of available bandwidth to it and ensuring low latency. An access list is used to identify the voice traffic.

Load Balancing is another crucial component of traffic engineering, especially in environments with high traffic volumes or multiple servers providing the same service. Load balancers distribute incoming traffic across multiple servers to ensure even distribution of the workload and prevent any single server from becoming a bottleneck.

To configure load balancing, organizations often deploy dedicated load balancer appliances or use software-based solutions. CLI commands or graphical user interfaces (GUIs) can be used to configure load balancing rules and policies.

For instance, configuring a basic round-robin load balancing algorithm on a load balancer might involve CLI commands like:

diffCopy code

serverfarm WEBFARM predictor roundrobin server SERVER1 weight 1 server SERVER2 weight 1 !

In this example, a server farm named WEBFARM is created with two servers, SERVER1 and SERVER2, assigned equal weights for round-robin load balancing.

Load balancers can also employ more advanced algorithms, such as Least Connections or Weighted Round Robin, to distribute traffic intelligently based on server health and capacity.

In addition to distributing traffic across servers, load balancers can perform various traffic optimization tasks, including SSL offloading, content caching, and compression, to enhance application performance.

Furthermore, Global Server Load Balancing (GSLB) allows organizations to distribute traffic across geographically dispersed data centers, ensuring high availability and disaster recovery. GSLB solutions often use DNS-based load balancing to direct clients to the nearest or most available data center.

To configure GSLB, organizations might use CLI commands to define DNS records and policies that route clients to the appropriate data center based on factors like proximity or server health.

Traffic Engineering also involves traffic shaping and bandwidth management. Traffic shaping techniques can be used to control the rate of data transmission on a network link, preventing network congestion and ensuring that critical traffic receives preferential treatment.

CLI commands can be used to configure traffic shaping on network devices. For instance:

kotlinCopy code

```
interface GigabitEthernet0/1 bandwidth 10000 traffic-shape rate 8000 !
```

In this example, the network interface is configured with a bandwidth of 10,000 Kbps, and traffic shaping is applied to limit outbound traffic to 8,000 Kbps.

Additionally, organizations may use Link Aggregation to increase network capacity and redundancy. Link Aggregation allows multiple physical links to be combined into a single logical link, providing greater bandwidth and fault tolerance.

CLI commands can be used to configure Link Aggregation on switches or routers.

Traffic Engineering also encompasses route optimization techniques, such as Traffic Engineering with Multiprotocol Label Switching (MPLS-TE). MPLS-TE allows network administrators to create explicit paths for traffic through the network, optimizing the routing of traffic and minimizing congestion.

CLI commands are used to configure MPLS-TE on routers. For instance:

kotlinCopy code

```
interface GigabitEthernet0/0 mpls traffic-eng tunnels !
```

In this example, the router interface is configured to enable MPLS traffic engineering tunnels.

Furthermore, organizations can leverage Software-Defined Networking (SDN) and programmable network devices to implement dynamic traffic engineering and load balancing policies based on real-time network conditions and application requirements.

Network administrators can use SDN controllers and APIs to configure traffic flows and load balancing rules dynamically, adapting to changing traffic patterns and network conditions.

In summary, Traffic Engineering and Load Balancing are essential aspects of network management that help organizations optimize their network resources, ensure efficient traffic flow, and enhance overall network performance. CLI commands play a crucial role in configuring and deploying these techniques, allowing network administrators to fine-tune network behavior to meet their specific requirements. Whether it's prioritizing critical traffic, distributing workloads across multiple servers, or shaping traffic flows, effective traffic engineering and load balancing are key to building a robust and responsive network infrastructure.

WAN Optimization and Acceleration Techniques are vital tools in modern networking that focus on improving the performance and efficiency of Wide Area Networks (WANs), enabling organizations to enhance productivity and reduce operational costs.

One of the primary challenges in WANs is latency, which can significantly impact the user experience, especially for applications that require real-time communication or data access. To address latency issues, WAN Optimization solutions often employ techniques like data compression and deduplication.

For example, to enable data compression on a WAN optimization device, administrators might use CLI commands like:

arduinoCopy code

```
compression algorithm deflate ! interface
GigabitEthernet0/0 compression max-header-size 50
```

In this example, the device is configured to use the "deflate" compression algorithm, reducing the size of data packets transmitted over the WAN. The "compression max-header-size" command sets the maximum header size for compressed packets.

Data deduplication is another essential technique used in WAN Optimization. It involves identifying and eliminating redundant data before transmitting it across the network. This reduces the amount of data that needs to be transferred, thereby saving bandwidth and reducing latency.

To configure data deduplication, administrators might use CLI commands like:

kotlinCopy code

```
deduplication enable ! interface GigabitEthernet0/0
deduplication max-sessions 1000
```

In this example, data deduplication is enabled on the WAN optimization device, and the "deduplication max-sessions" command sets the maximum number of deduplication sessions.

WAN Optimization devices also often employ protocol optimization techniques to improve the performance of specific applications and protocols. For instance, WAN optimization solutions can optimize the performance of CIFS/SMB (Common Internet File System/Server Message Block) for efficient file sharing over the WAN.

CLI commands may be used to configure protocol optimization policies. For example:
bashCopy code

```
protocol-optimization cifs enable !
```

This command enables CIFS protocol optimization on the WAN optimization device, allowing it to optimize the transfer of files and data between remote locations.

Caching is another crucial WAN optimization technique that helps reduce latency and accelerate data access for frequently used content. WAN optimization devices can cache content locally, ensuring that users can access it quickly without repeatedly fetching data from the central data center.

To configure caching, administrators may use CLI commands to specify caching policies and storage settings. For example:
luaCopy code

```
cache policy content match url-prefix /images/ storage local-disk !
```

In this example, a caching policy is defined to match URLs with the "/images/" prefix and store cached content on the local disk of the WAN optimization device.

Furthermore, WAN optimization and acceleration techniques often include Quality of Service (QoS) mechanisms to prioritize critical traffic over less important data. This ensures that mission-critical applications receive the necessary bandwidth and latency guarantees.

To configure QoS for WAN optimization, administrators may use CLI commands to define traffic classes and policies. For instance:
pythonCopy code

```
class-map match-any voice match access-group 101 !
policy-map QoS class voice priority percent 30 class
class-default fair-queue ! interface GigabitEthernet0/0
```

service-policy output QoS ! access-list 101 permit udp any any range 16384 32767

In this example, a QoS policy is defined to prioritize voice traffic based on an access list that identifies UDP traffic in a specific port range.

Additionally, WAN optimization solutions often offer application acceleration features that optimize the performance of specific applications, such as Microsoft Exchange or SharePoint. These features may involve protocol optimizations, compression, and content caching tailored to the needs of the particular application.

Organizations can also employ WAN optimization techniques like traffic shaping to control the rate of data transmission across the WAN links, ensuring that critical traffic receives preferential treatment while non-essential traffic is limited.

CLI commands can be used to configure traffic shaping policies on WAN optimization devices. For example:

kotlinCopy code

interface GigabitEthernet0/1 bandwidth 10000 traffic-shape rate 8000

In this example, the interface is configured with a bandwidth of 10,000 Kbps, and traffic shaping is applied to limit outbound traffic to 8,000 Kbps.

Lastly, organizations may choose to implement Software-Defined WAN (SD-WAN) solutions, which combine WAN optimization techniques with dynamic traffic routing to enhance network performance further.

SD-WAN solutions often use CLI commands or graphical interfaces to configure traffic routing policies based on real-time network conditions and application requirements.

In summary, WAN Optimization and Acceleration Techniques are essential for improving the performance and efficiency of Wide Area Networks. These techniques include data compression, deduplication, protocol optimization, caching, QoS, and application acceleration. CLI commands are commonly used to configure these techniques on WAN optimization devices, allowing organizations to optimize their WAN infrastructure for maximum efficiency and user satisfaction.

## BOOK 4
## EXPERT TCP/IP OPTIMIZATION AND TROUBLESHOOTING

### ROB BOTWRIGHT

## Chapter 1: Advanced Network Analysis and Troubleshooting

Deep Packet Inspection (DPI) tools are a critical component of modern network management and security strategies, providing a comprehensive and detailed analysis of network traffic for a wide range of applications and purposes.

These tools enable network administrators and security professionals to gain granular insights into the traffic traversing their networks, facilitating efficient management, security enforcement, and troubleshooting. DPI goes beyond conventional packet inspection by examining the content and context of data packets, making it a powerful asset for various network-related tasks.

To deploy DPI effectively, organizations can utilize dedicated DPI appliances or software solutions that can be integrated into existing network infrastructure. These tools often employ a combination of hardware and software components to capture, inspect, and analyze network packets in real-time.

DPI tools are particularly useful for network security, as they can identify and mitigate various threats, such as malware, intrusion attempts, and data exfiltration. For example, they can detect known malware signatures, anomalous traffic patterns, and malicious payloads within packets.

Intrusion Detection Systems (IDS) and Intrusion Prevention Systems (IPS) are common security applications that rely on DPI to monitor network traffic for suspicious activities. When malicious behavior is detected, these systems can take proactive measures, such as blocking or alerting network administrators.

To configure an IDS/IPS using DPI, administrators can employ CLI commands like:

pythonCopy code

```
configure terminal ! class-map type inspect match-any
malware match protocol http match protocol smtp match
protocol ftp ! policy-map type inspect http-malware-policy
class type inspect malware drop-connection log ! zone
security internet zone security internal ! zone-pair security
internet-to-internal source internet destination internal
service-policy type inspect http-malware-policy ! interface
GigabitEthernet0/0 zone-member security internet !
interface GigabitEthernet0/1 zone-member security
internal ! end
```

In this example, a policy map is defined to inspect HTTP, SMTP, and FTP traffic for malware using DPI. When malware is detected, the connection is dropped, and a log entry is generated.

DPI tools also play a crucial role in Quality of Service (QoS) management, allowing organizations to prioritize specific applications or traffic types over others to ensure optimal performance. By analyzing packet content and headers, DPI can identify applications and apply QoS policies accordingly.

To configure QoS using DPI, administrators might use CLI commands like:

pythonCopy code

```
class-map match-any voice match access-group 101 !
policy-map QoS class voice priority percent 30 class
class-default fair-queue ! interface GigabitEthernet0/0
service-policy output QoS ! access-list 101 permit udp any
any range 16384 32767
```

In this scenario, a QoS policy is created to prioritize voice traffic based on an access list that identifies UDP traffic within a specific port range.

Furthermore, DPI tools can be leveraged for bandwidth management and optimization. By analyzing traffic patterns and data usage, organizations can identify bandwidth-hungry applications or users and take appropriate actions, such as traffic shaping or bandwidth allocation.

To configure bandwidth management with DPI, administrators may use CLI commands to set bandwidth limits or create traffic shaping policies tailored to specific applications or users.

DPI is not limited to security and QoS; it also serves as a valuable asset for network troubleshooting. It provides visibility into network performance issues, helping administrators pinpoint the root causes of problems and optimize network resources effectively.

To troubleshoot network issues with DPI, administrators can utilize DPI logs and analysis tools to identify abnormal traffic patterns, network congestion, or misconfigured applications. They can then make informed decisions to address these issues and improve network reliability.

Additionally, DPI is instrumental in compliance monitoring and reporting, as it allows organizations to track and audit data flows to ensure compliance with industry regulations and internal policies. DPI can help identify unauthorized data transfers, potential data leaks, or violations of acceptable use policies.

To deploy DPI for compliance monitoring, organizations can create policies and alerts based on specific keywords or data patterns found within network packets. When DPI identifies potential violations, it can trigger alerts or log entries for further investigation and action.

In summary, Deep Packet Inspection (DPI) tools are essential components of modern network management and security. They enable granular network traffic analysis, facilitating security enforcement, quality of service management, bandwidth optimization, troubleshooting, and compliance monitoring. DPI tools can be deployed using dedicated appliances or software solutions and are configurable through CLI commands, helping organizations achieve enhanced network visibility and control.

Network anomaly detection techniques play a vital role in modern network security, helping organizations identify and respond to suspicious or abnormal activities within their network environments. These techniques are designed to detect deviations from expected network behavior, which can be indicative of security threats, operational issues, or performance problems.

Deploying network anomaly detection techniques effectively requires a comprehensive understanding of the network's normal behavior and a variety of tools and methodologies. One common approach is to use intrusion detection systems (IDS) and intrusion prevention systems (IPS), which can incorporate anomaly detection capabilities.

To configure an IDS/IPS with anomaly detection, network administrators can employ CLI commands like:

pythonCopy code

```
configure terminal ! class-map type inspect match-any
anomalous-traffic match protocol icmp match protocol udp
match protocol tcp ! policy-map type inspect anomalous-
traffic-policy class type inspect anomalous-traffic drop-
connection log ! zone security internet zone security
internal ! zone-pair security internet-to-internal source
internet destination internal service-policy type inspect
```

anomalous-traffic-policy ! interface GigabitEthernet0/0 zone-member security internet ! interface GigabitEthernet0/1 zone-member security internal ! end

In this example, a policy map is defined to inspect ICMP, UDP, and TCP traffic for anomalies. When anomalous traffic is detected, the connection is dropped, and a log entry is generated.

Another effective technique for network anomaly detection is statistical analysis. This approach involves establishing baseline behavior patterns for the network and then continuously monitoring and comparing incoming traffic against these baselines. Any deviations beyond acceptable thresholds are flagged as anomalies.

Statistical analysis tools can utilize CLI commands to set up and adjust baseline parameters, such as traffic volume, bandwidth utilization, and packet patterns, to adapt to changing network conditions.

Machine learning and artificial intelligence (AI) are increasingly being employed for network anomaly detection. These technologies can analyze large volumes of network data, identify subtle patterns, and detect anomalies that may be challenging to spot using traditional methods.

To deploy machine learning-based anomaly detection, organizations can utilize specialized software solutions that require configuration and fine-tuning. CLI commands may be used to set parameters, such as training data sources, algorithm selection, and alert thresholds.

Behavioral analysis is another valuable technique that focuses on understanding the typical behavior of users and devices within a network. By monitoring user activities and device interactions, behavioral analysis can detect deviations from established patterns, such as unusual login times, access to unauthorized resources, or changes in data transfer patterns.

To implement behavioral analysis, organizations may rely on security information and event management (SIEM) systems that use CLI commands for customization and integration with other security tools.

Flow-based analysis is a technique that examines network traffic flows, providing insights into the communication patterns between devices and systems. Flow data can include information about source and destination IP addresses, ports, protocols, and duration of connections.

To leverage flow-based analysis, organizations can use flow monitoring tools that collect and analyze flow data. CLI commands may be used to configure flow collectors, specify flow export protocols, and set flow analysis parameters.

Packet capture and analysis is a fundamental technique for network anomaly detection, as it involves capturing and inspecting individual network packets in real-time. Packet analyzers can help identify anomalies, such as malformed packets, excessive traffic from specific sources, or unusual packet patterns.

Administrators can deploy packet capture and analysis tools by configuring packet capture filters and triggers using CLI commands. These tools can be instrumental in diagnosing network performance issues and identifying potential security threats.

Furthermore, signature-based detection techniques are widely used for identifying known patterns of malicious activity. Security tools and devices, such as antivirus software, intrusion detection systems, and firewalls, utilize signature databases to compare incoming network traffic against known attack signatures.

To enable signature-based detection, organizations can update signature databases regularly and configure security devices with appropriate CLI commands to enforce signature-based policies.

Network anomaly detection techniques are not limited to security applications; they can also be beneficial for network performance management. By identifying abnormal traffic patterns, bottlenecks, or misconfigurations, organizations can optimize their network resources and enhance overall network performance.

In summary, network anomaly detection techniques are essential components of a comprehensive network security strategy. These techniques encompass various approaches, including intrusion detection, statistical analysis, machine learning, behavioral analysis, flow-based analysis, packet capture and analysis, and signature-based detection. Deploying these techniques effectively often involves configuring security tools, monitoring systems, and analyzing network data using CLI commands and specialized software solutions. By leveraging network anomaly detection, organizations can bolster their security posture, detect and mitigate threats, and improve network performance and reliability.

## Chapter 2: Performance Tuning Techniques

Optimization of bandwidth utilization is a critical concern for organizations of all sizes, as it directly impacts network performance, cost efficiency, and user satisfaction. In today's digital age, where data flows continuously across networks, efficiently managing and optimizing available bandwidth is more important than ever.

One fundamental aspect of bandwidth optimization involves understanding the traffic patterns on your network. It's essential to have a clear picture of which applications and services are consuming the most bandwidth, as this information informs your optimization strategies.

To gain insight into traffic patterns, network administrators can employ network monitoring and analysis tools. These tools allow you to identify the top bandwidth-consuming applications and services, which may include video streaming, file downloads, cloud-based applications, and more.

Once you've identified bandwidth-hungry applications, you can implement quality of service (QoS) mechanisms to prioritize critical traffic. QoS allows you to allocate more bandwidth to mission-critical applications while limiting the bandwidth available to less important or non-essential traffic.

To configure QoS, you can use CLI commands on network devices such as routers and switches. For example:

arduinoCopy code

```
configure terminal ! class-map match-any critical-traffic
match protocol http match protocol voip ! policy-map QoS-
policy class critical-traffic bandwidth percent 70 class
```

class-default fair-queue ! interface GigabitEthernet0/0 service-policy output QoS-policy ! end

In this example, a QoS policy is defined to prioritize HTTP and VoIP traffic, allocating 70% of the available bandwidth to critical traffic and employing fair queuing for other traffic classes.

Bandwidth optimization also involves minimizing network congestion. Congestion occurs when network resources, such as links or switches, become overwhelmed by the volume of traffic. To address congestion, administrators can implement techniques like traffic shaping and traffic policing. Traffic shaping smooths traffic flows by buffering and controlling the rate at which packets are sent. On the other hand, traffic policing drops or marks excessive traffic to prevent it from congesting the network.

To configure traffic shaping, you can use CLI commands like this:

vbnetCopy code

configure terminal ! policy-map shaping-policy class class-default shape average 1000000 ! interface GigabitEthernet0/0 service-policy output shaping-policy ! end

In this example, a policy map is defined to shape traffic to an average rate of 1 Mbps on the specified interface.

Bandwidth optimization also involves managing multicast and broadcast traffic efficiently. Excessive multicast or broadcast traffic can consume a significant portion of available bandwidth, causing network congestion.

Administrators can use CLI commands to configure multicast routing protocols, such as Protocol Independent Multicast (PIM), to control multicast traffic. Additionally, network segmentation and VLANs can help isolate broadcast domains and limit the spread of broadcast traffic.

Another critical aspect of bandwidth optimization is the deployment of content delivery networks (CDNs) and caching solutions. CDNs distribute content closer to end-users, reducing the need for data to traverse long distances across the network. Caching stores frequently accessed content locally, reducing the repetitive transfer of the same data over the network.

To deploy a CDN or caching solution, organizations can work with CDN providers and configure their network to direct traffic to CDN servers. This often involves updating DNS records and using load balancing techniques.

Furthermore, bandwidth optimization includes the use of compression and optimization technologies. Data compression reduces the size of data packets transmitted over the network, effectively conserving bandwidth. Various CLI commands can be used to enable compression on network devices and adjust compression settings to balance between compression ratio and CPU usage.

Additionally, content optimization techniques, such as content delivery acceleration (CDA) and web acceleration, can be applied to reduce the latency associated with loading web content. These optimizations can be achieved through specialized hardware or software solutions, often requiring specific CLI configurations.

It's important to consider the impact of security measures on bandwidth utilization. While security measures, such as firewall rules and intrusion detection systems, are crucial for network protection, they can also consume bandwidth when inspecting traffic.

Administrators can configure security devices to strike a balance between thorough inspection and efficient bandwidth utilization. This may involve optimizing firewall rules, tuning intrusion detection system settings, and implementing intrusion prevention mechanisms to reduce the impact of security measures on bandwidth.

Moreover, bandwidth optimization extends to network design considerations. Organizations can implement strategies like link aggregation and redundancy to ensure that critical traffic always has a path to follow, even in the event of link failures. CLI commands can be used to configure link aggregation protocols like Link Aggregation Control Protocol (LACP) to optimize bandwidth utilization across multiple links.

Additionally, implementing a well-structured hierarchical network design can enhance bandwidth utilization. This design separates the network into core, distribution, and access layers, allowing for efficient traffic management and optimized bandwidth allocation. CLI commands are essential for configuring the various network devices and routing protocols needed for this design.

In summary, bandwidth optimization is a multifaceted endeavor that requires a combination of techniques, tools, and careful configuration using CLI commands. By monitoring traffic patterns, implementing QoS, managing congestion, deploying CDNs and caching solutions, leveraging compression and content optimization, and considering security measures and network design, organizations can make the most of their available bandwidth, ensuring optimal network performance and cost-effectiveness.

Advanced server and application performance tuning is a critical aspect of managing modern IT environments, where the efficient operation of servers and applications is paramount. Organizations rely on their servers and applications to deliver services, support business processes, and meet customer demands. Therefore, optimizing their performance is essential to ensure a smooth and responsive computing experience.

One fundamental aspect of performance tuning is monitoring the server's resource utilization. To gain insight into a server's performance, administrators can employ various monitoring tools and CLI commands that provide real-time and historical data on CPU usage, memory usage, disk I/O, and network activity.

For example, in a Linux environment, the "top" command provides a dynamic view of system processes and resource utilization. By running "top" in the command line, administrators can quickly identify resource-hungry processes and take appropriate actions, such as optimizing configurations or allocating additional resources.

Disk I/O is a common bottleneck in server performance. To address this, administrators can implement techniques such as RAID (Redundant Array of Independent Disks) to improve both performance and fault tolerance. CLI commands are used to configure RAID levels, such as RAID 0, RAID 1, or RAID 5, depending on the desired balance between performance and redundancy.

Additionally, the choice of storage technology, such as SSDs (Solid-State Drives) versus traditional HDDs (Hard Disk Drives), plays a crucial role in server performance. SSDs offer significantly faster read and write speeds, reducing latency and improving overall application responsiveness. By choosing the appropriate storage technology and configuring it correctly, administrators can enhance server performance.

In virtualized environments, resource allocation is a key consideration. Administrators can use hypervisor management tools and CLI commands to adjust the allocation of CPU cores, memory, and disk space to virtual machines (VMs). Ensuring that VMs receive adequate resources helps prevent resource contention and ensures optimal application performance.

Memory optimization is another critical aspect of server performance tuning. Techniques like memory caching and swapping can significantly impact server responsiveness. By configuring memory caching using CLI commands, administrators can speed up access to frequently used data, reducing the need to fetch data from slower storage devices. Moreover, server operating systems often provide performance optimization features that can be leveraged through CLI commands or graphical interfaces. For instance, Windows Server includes the "Performance Options" settings that allow administrators to fine-tune system performance by adjusting settings related to processor scheduling, memory usage, and file caching.

In addition to server tuning, optimizing application performance is equally important. Applications can be resource-intensive and may require specific configurations to operate efficiently. Administrators can use profiling tools and CLI commands to identify application bottlenecks and performance issues.

Database performance is a critical concern for many applications. Tuning database servers involves optimizing queries, indexing, and caching mechanisms. Database administrators can use SQL queries and statements to optimize database performance, which may include creating appropriate indexes, rewriting inefficient queries, and adjusting database configuration parameters.

Furthermore, web applications often benefit from caching mechanisms to reduce the load on application servers and improve response times. Technologies like Content Delivery Networks (CDNs) can be deployed to cache and serve static content, while application-level caching can be configured through CLI commands or application settings.

Load balancing is a common technique used to distribute incoming traffic across multiple servers, improving both performance and fault tolerance. Load balancers can be configured using CLI commands to evenly distribute requests among servers, ensuring efficient resource utilization and high availability.

Server and application performance tuning also extends to security considerations. Administrators must strike a balance between optimizing performance and implementing security measures. Security CLI commands can be used to configure firewalls, intrusion detection systems, and other security tools, ensuring that they do not unnecessarily impact server or application performance.

Moreover, advanced performance tuning may involve optimizing network configurations, such as adjusting TCP/IP settings to reduce latency and improve throughput. CLI commands can be employed to fine-tune network parameters, ensuring that data flows efficiently between servers and clients.

In summary, advanced server and application performance tuning require a holistic approach that encompasses monitoring, resource allocation, storage optimization, memory management, database tuning, caching mechanisms, load balancing, security measures, and network optimization. CLI commands play a crucial role in configuring and fine-tuning various aspects of servers and applications to ensure optimal performance and responsiveness, ultimately delivering a superior computing experience for users and customers alike.

## Chapter 3: Network Traffic Analysis and Packet Capture

Wireshark is a powerful network protocol analyzer that allows network administrators and security professionals to capture, inspect, and analyze network traffic in real-time. It provides deep insights into the communication between devices on a network, helping diagnose network issues, troubleshoot problems, and detect security threats.

To initiate packet capturing with Wireshark, open the application and select the network interface you want to monitor from the list of available interfaces. Typically, you can do this by clicking on "Capture" in the top menu and choosing the desired interface. For example, if you want to capture traffic on your Ethernet adapter, you might select "Ethernet" or "eth0."

Once capturing begins, Wireshark displays a live stream of packets flowing through the selected interface. Each packet is listed in the main window, showing details like source and destination IP addresses, protocols used, packet length, and a timestamp.

To focus on specific packets of interest, you can apply filters using Wireshark's display filter field. For instance, to view only HTTP traffic, you can enter "http" in the filter field. This allows you to isolate and analyze the HTTP packets within the captured data.

Packet analysis often involves examining packet contents in detail. By selecting a specific packet in the list, you can expand its tree view to explore individual layers of the packet. This is where Wireshark truly shines, as it decodes and displays the content of each packet, including application-layer data.

For example, if you're troubleshooting a web application issue, you can select an HTTP packet and inspect its contents to see the HTTP request and response headers. This information can reveal potential problems, such as incorrect headers or missing data.

Beyond simple packet inspection, Wireshark provides advanced features for in-depth analysis. One such feature is the ability to follow a TCP stream. By right-clicking on a TCP packet and selecting "Follow," you can reconstruct the entire conversation between two devices. This is particularly useful for understanding the sequence of requests and responses in complex transactions.

Wireshark also offers statistical analysis tools that can help identify patterns and anomalies in network traffic. For example, the "Statistics" menu provides various options for generating reports on packet counts, protocol distribution, and endpoint conversations.

Additionally, you can leverage Wireshark's expert system, which highlights potential issues and provides explanations. When Wireshark detects a problem, it adds entries to the "Expert Info" section, indicating issues such as duplicate ACKs, retransmissions, or out-of-order packets.

Advanced users can further enhance their analysis with custom Lua scripts. Wireshark supports scripting using Lua, enabling you to create custom dissectors and filters tailored to your specific needs. These scripts can automate repetitive tasks and extract specific information from packets.

In the context of network troubleshooting, Wireshark can assist in identifying problems related to network configuration, latency, and packet loss. For example, by analyzing the time it takes for packets to traverse the network (round-trip time), you can pinpoint areas where latency is a concern.

Wireshark can also reveal the presence of packet loss or retransmissions, which may indicate network congestion or reliability issues. This information is invaluable for diagnosing performance problems and optimizing network infrastructure.

From a security perspective, Wireshark aids in detecting suspicious or malicious activity on the network. By analyzing packet payloads, you can uncover signs of intrusion attempts, malware communication, or data breaches. For example, unusual patterns in DNS requests or unexpected traffic from specific IP addresses may raise red flags.

Moreover, Wireshark is a valuable tool for incident response and forensic analysis. Security professionals can use it to reconstruct and analyze the details of a security incident, such as a data breach or a malware infection. Wireshark captures a chronological record of network traffic, allowing investigators to piece together the events leading up to and following the incident.

To summarize, Wireshark is an indispensable tool for network administrators, security experts, and anyone involved in network analysis. Its ability to capture, dissect, and analyze packets in real-time provides essential insights into network performance and security. By leveraging its features, including display filters, protocol decoding, stream following, statistical analysis, expert system, Lua scripting, and more, users can efficiently troubleshoot network issues, detect security threats, and conduct in-depth packet analysis for various purposes. Whether you're managing a complex enterprise network, investigating security incidents, or optimizing network performance, Wireshark is an invaluable asset in your toolkit.

In the realm of network management and security, advanced traffic analysis tools and methods have become indispensable for professionals seeking to gain deeper insights into their network's behavior, identify anomalies, troubleshoot issues, and enhance overall performance.

One such advanced tool is Zeek (formerly known as Bro), a powerful network security monitoring framework. Zeek operates passively, observing network traffic as it flows across the wire, making it a valuable asset for intrusion detection, network forensics, and traffic analysis.

To deploy Zeek, you can start by installing it on a dedicated machine within your network. Once installed, you configure Zeek to monitor specific network interfaces by editing its configuration file. For instance, you can specify which subnets or IP ranges to monitor, which protocols to capture, and where to store the collected data.

Zeek's real strength lies in its ability to extract high-level information from raw network traffic. It dissects network packets, identifies protocols, extracts content, and generates structured logs. Analysts can then use these logs to gain insights into network activity.

The command-line interface (CLI) plays a crucial role in using Zeek effectively. By running Zeek scripts and commands, you can initiate packet capturing, start log analysis, and generate reports. For example, to analyze HTTP traffic, you can run the "bro-cut" command with appropriate filters to extract HTTP-related data from Zeek logs.

Another advanced traffic analysis tool is Suricata, an open-source Network IDS, IPS, and Network Security Monitoring (NSM) engine. Suricata is capable of inspecting network traffic at high speeds and detecting a wide range of threats and anomalies.

To deploy Suricata, you need to install it on a dedicated server or sensor within your network. Similar to Zeek, you configure Suricata by editing its configuration file to specify the network interfaces to monitor and the rules to apply for traffic inspection.

Suricata's CLI is essential for managing and utilizing the tool effectively. You can start Suricata with specific configuration options and rulesets to target your network's security and monitoring needs. For example, you can use the "suricata -c" command to specify the configuration file and "suricata-update" to update the rules.

Advanced traffic analysis often involves examining network flows and connections comprehensively. Flow analysis tools, like ntopng, provide an in-depth view of network traffic by tracking the conversations between devices.

To set up ntopng, you can install it on a server within your network and configure it to monitor the desired network interfaces. Once operational, ntopng presents network flows and connections in an intuitive web-based interface.

The CLI can be used to manage ntopng's configuration and perform specific tasks. For instance, you can restart the ntopng service, specify which interfaces to monitor, or set up alerts for particular traffic patterns.

Flow analysis tools also offer advanced features, such as the ability to drill down into individual flows, identify top talkers on the network, and visualize traffic patterns over time. These capabilities are invaluable for pinpointing performance bottlenecks, identifying bandwidth hogs, and detecting unusual behavior.

Wireshark, while known for its packet-level analysis capabilities, also provides advanced features for traffic analysis. Wireshark's Conversations feature allows you to view statistics and details about network conversations, such as the number of packets exchanged, data transferred, and duration of the conversation.

To access this feature in Wireshark, navigate to the "Statistics" menu, choose "Conversations," and select the appropriate network interface. Wireshark will then display a table of network conversations, organized by protocols, with associated statistics.

By examining network conversations, you can gain insights into which devices are communicating most frequently, the protocols they use, and the volume of data exchanged. This information can help you identify traffic patterns, potential issues, or unusual activity on your network.

Advanced traffic analysis extends beyond the tools themselves and encompasses the methods and strategies employed by network professionals. One method involves the use of baselines, which are established patterns of normal network behavior. By creating baselines for your network, you can better detect deviations and anomalies.

CLI commands for baseline analysis often involve using tools like tcpdump or tshark to capture packets for a predefined period while the network is operating normally. These captured packets can serve as a reference for identifying abnormal behavior when analyzing future traffic.

Additionally, statistical analysis tools like R or Python can be used to process and visualize network data for trend analysis. You can generate graphs and charts to highlight variations in network traffic over time, making it easier to spot irregularities.

Another advanced method is the use of machine learning and anomaly detection algorithms. By training models on historical network data, you can build classifiers that can automatically flag unusual behavior. These models can be applied to real-time traffic analysis to identify potential threats or issues.

In summary, advanced traffic analysis tools and methods are essential for gaining deeper insights into network behavior, detecting anomalies, and ensuring the security and performance of your network infrastructure. Tools like Zeek, Suricata, ntopng, and Wireshark, combined with CLI commands and statistical analysis techniques, empower network professionals to proactively manage their networks, detect security threats, and optimize performance effectively. Incorporating these tools and methods into your network management and security practices will help you stay ahead in the ever-evolving world of networking.

## Chapter 4: Advanced Routing Protocols and Optimization

In the world of advanced networking, OSPF (Open Shortest Path First) and EIGRP (Enhanced Interior Gateway Routing Protocol) are two widely used routing protocols that play a crucial role in designing and managing complex network infrastructures. As network engineers delve deeper into these protocols, they often encounter scenarios that require advanced configurations and optimizations to ensure efficient routing, redundancy, and scalability.

One of the advanced techniques in OSPF configuration is the use of OSPF Areas. OSPF divides a network into logical areas, known as OSPF areas, to simplify routing and reduce the size of the OSPF topology database. By segmenting the network into areas, engineers can control the propagation of routing information, minimize the impact of topology changes, and improve network convergence.

To deploy OSPF areas, you can configure routers within the same area to establish OSPF neighbor relationships and exchange routing information. For example, you can use the following CLI command to configure OSPF on a Cisco router:

scssCopy code

Router(config)# router ospf [process-id]  Router(config-router)# network [network-address] [wildcard-mask] area [area-id]

In this command, you specify the OSPF process ID, network addresses, wildcard masks, and the area ID to determine which interfaces participate in OSPF routing within a specific area.

Another advanced OSPF feature is the implementation of OSPF Virtual Links. Virtual Links are used to connect OSPF areas when a non-backbone area is not directly connected to the OSPF backbone area (Area 0). This can occur in scenarios where a physical link to the backbone area is unavailable, and a virtual link serves as a workaround.

To configure an OSPF Virtual Link, you need to specify the router IDs of the two routers at either end of the virtual link. For instance, you can use the following CLI command to configure a virtual link between two OSPF routers:

scssCopy code

Router(config)# router ospf [process-id] Router(config-router)# area [area-id] virtual-link [neighbor-router-id]

This command establishes a virtual link between the specified routers, allowing traffic to flow between non-backbone areas and the backbone area through this virtual connection.

EIGRP, on the other hand, offers advanced capabilities such as route summarization and route filtering. Route summarization, also known as route aggregation, involves consolidating multiple network prefixes into a single, summarized route advertisement. This can significantly reduce the size of the routing table and improve network efficiency.

To configure route summarization in EIGRP, you can use the following CLI command on a Cisco router:

scssCopy code

Router(config)# router eigrp [AS-number] Router(config-router)# summary-address [summary-network] [mask]

In this command, you specify the EIGRP autonomous system (AS) number, the summary network, and the associated mask. This tells the router to advertise the summarized route instead of individual subnets, reducing the number of entries in the routing table.

Route filtering in EIGRP allows network engineers to control which routes are advertised or accepted by EIGRP routers. This can be useful for security, route optimization, and controlling traffic flow within the network.

To implement route filtering in EIGRP, you can configure access control lists (ACLs) or distribute lists to permit or deny specific routes. For example, you can use the following CLI command to filter routes based on an ACL in EIGRP:

scssCopy code

```
Router(config)# router eigrp [AS-number] Router(config-router)# distribute-list [ACL-number] [in|out] [interface]
```

In this command, you specify the EIGRP AS number, the ACL number, and whether the filtering should be applied on incoming or outgoing routes. The interface parameter can further narrow down the application of the filter to a specific interface.

Advanced configurations also involve EIGRP summarization techniques. Summarization in EIGRP can be done at multiple points within the network to optimize routing table size and reduce unnecessary route advertisements.

To configure EIGRP summarization, you can use the following CLI command on a Cisco router:

scssCopy code

```
Router(config)# interface [interface-type] [interface-number] Router(config-if)# ip summary-address eigrp [AS-number] [summary-network] [mask]
```

This command is applied to the interface where you want to perform summarization. It allows you to specify the EIGRP AS number, the summary network, and the mask for summarization on that interface.

In advanced OSPF and EIGRP configurations, engineers may also explore route redistribution techniques. Route redistribution involves the exchange of routing information between different routing protocols, allowing networks using different protocols to interoperate.

To perform route redistribution, you can use the "redistribute" command in the routing protocol configuration mode. For example, to redistribute routes from EIGRP into OSPF, you can use the following CLI command on a Cisco router running OSPF:

scssCopy code

Router(config)# router ospf [process-id] Router(config-router)# redistribute eigrp [AS-number] subnets

In this command, you specify the OSPF process ID, the EIGRP AS number, and the "subnets" keyword to redistribute EIGRP routes into OSPF.

In summary, advanced OSPF and EIGRP configurations involve techniques such as OSPF areas, virtual links, EIGRP route summarization, route filtering, and route redistribution. These techniques allow network engineers to optimize routing, enhance network scalability, and control the flow of routing information within complex network environments. By mastering these advanced configurations and understanding when and how to deploy them, network professionals can build robust, efficient, and highly adaptable networks that meet the demands of modern communication.

BGP (Border Gateway Protocol) is a critical routing protocol used in the Internet and large-scale networks to facilitate the exchange of routing and reachability information among autonomous systems (ASes). As networks grow and become more complex, optimizing BGP becomes essential to ensure efficient routing, minimize convergence times, and maintain network stability.

One common BGP optimization strategy is the use of route aggregation. Aggregation involves combining multiple IP prefixes into a single, summarized route announcement. This reduces the size of BGP routing tables and minimizes the number of updates exchanged between BGP routers. Route aggregation is typically implemented using the "aggregate-address" command in BGP configuration.

For instance, on a Cisco router, you can use the following CLI command to aggregate routes in BGP:

scssCopy code

```
Router(config-router)# aggregate-address [prefix] [prefix-length] [summary-only]
```

In this command, you specify the IP prefix to be aggregated, its prefix length, and whether you want to generate a summary route only. By aggregating routes, BGP routers advertise a single prefix that covers a range of smaller prefixes, which is especially useful when dealing with numerous subnets.

Another crucial optimization technique is BGP route filtering. By filtering BGP routes, network administrators can control which routes are accepted or advertised, enhancing security and reducing unnecessary routing information propagation.

To filter BGP routes, you can use the "distribute-list" or "prefix-list" commands in BGP configuration. For example, to filter routes based on a prefix list, you can use the following CLI command:

scssCopy code

```
Router(config-router)# neighbor [neighbor-address] prefix-list [prefix-list-name] in
```

Here, you specify the neighbor's address, the prefix list name, and the direction (inbound or outbound) in which the filter should be applied. Prefix lists contain rules that define which routes should be permitted or denied based on specific criteria, such as prefix length or AS path.

Additionally, BGP route manipulation can be achieved using the "route-map" feature. Route maps allow you to modify attributes of BGP routes, such as the AS path, next-hop IP address, or local preference.

To create and apply a route map in BGP, you can use commands like:

scssCopy code

Router(config)# route-map [route-map-name] permit [sequence-number] Router(config-route-map)# match ip address [access-list-name] Router(config-route-map)# set as-path prepend [AS-number]

In this example, you create a route map, specify the match criteria using an access list, and set the AS path to prepend your AS number to incoming routes. This technique can be useful for influencing traffic engineering and route selection.

BGP also offers the capability to influence routing decisions through the manipulation of BGP attributes like the weight, local preference, and MED (Multi-Exit Discriminator). For instance, to assign a higher weight to a specific route, you can use the "weight" command in BGP configuration:

scssCopy code

Router(config-router)# neighbor [neighbor-address] weight [weight-value]

By adjusting these attributes, network administrators can control the preferred path for outbound traffic and influence BGP routers' routing decisions.

Additionally, BGP communities provide a way to tag routes with community values, allowing for more granular control over route propagation and policies. By attaching community values to routes, network operators can apply specific policies based on those values using route maps.

To apply a BGP community value, you can use the "set community" command within a route map:

```
arduinoCopy code
```
Router(config-route-map)# set community [community-value] additive

The "additive" keyword allows you to append the community value to the existing community attributes. By doing so, you can signal specific policies or preferences to other BGP routers.

BGP route dampening is another optimization technique aimed at mitigating the impact of route instability or flapping. Route dampening penalizes routes that frequently change state by increasing the route's route metric, making it less attractive to route selection.

To enable BGP route dampening, you can use the following CLI command:

```
arduinoCopy code
```
Router(config-router)# bgp dampening

By configuring route dampening parameters, such as the half-life and reuse timers, network administrators can fine-tune the dampening process to suit their network's stability requirements.

Another optimization strategy in BGP is the implementation of route reflection. In large BGP networks with multiple routers, full mesh peerings can become impractical. Route reflection allows for hierarchical BGP route distribution, reducing the complexity of BGP mesh topologies and improving scalability.

To configure BGP route reflection, you designate certain routers as route reflectors and configure others as clients. Route reflectors reflect BGP route information to clients, reducing the number of peerings required.

In BGP route reflector configuration, you can use commands like:

```
scssCopy code
```

Router(config-router)# neighbor [route-reflector-address] route-reflector-client

This command designates a neighbor as a route reflector client, instructing it to receive routes from the route reflector.

Furthermore, BGP optimization encompasses the deployment of route summarization techniques. Summarization reduces the number of BGP routes announced to neighbors by aggregating routes within a given prefix range. This helps minimize routing table size and simplifies routing.

To summarize BGP routes, you can use commands like: scssCopy code

Router(config-router)# aggregate-address [prefix] [prefix-length] [summary-only]

Here, you specify the prefix to be summarized and its prefix length, along with an option to generate a summary route only.

Lastly, BGP communities can be used extensively for traffic engineering purposes. By attaching specific community values to routes, network operators can signal their intent to peer networks or service providers. This enables fine-grained control over how traffic is routed and manipulated.

In BGP community-based traffic engineering, you can use the "set community" command within a route map to assign community values to routes. For example:

arduinoCopy code

Router(config-route-map)# set community [community-value] additive

By applying this technique, BGP communities can help manage traffic flows, optimize route selection, and enforce network policies effectively.

**Chapter 5: Security Hardening and Intrusion Detection**

Advanced firewall configuration plays a pivotal role in modern network security, offering enhanced protection against evolving cyber threats and tailored defense mechanisms for specific network environments. Next, we delve into the intricacies of advanced firewall configurations, exploring techniques, strategies, and CLI commands to fortify your network defenses.

One of the fundamental components of advanced firewall configuration is the use of Access Control Lists (ACLs). ACLs serve as the building blocks for defining traffic policies, specifying what is allowed and what is denied at the network perimeter. They can be configured at both the ingress and egress points of a network, providing granular control over traffic flows.

To create an ACL, you can use the following Cisco IOS CLI command:

scssCopy code

Router(config)# access-list [number] [permit | deny] [source] [destination] [protocol]

Here, you specify the ACL number, the action (permit or deny), source and destination IP addresses, and the protocol. By crafting precise ACLs, you can permit or deny traffic based on criteria such as source and destination IP addresses, port numbers, and protocol types.

Furthermore, advanced firewall configurations often involve the implementation of stateful packet inspection (SPI) or stateful inspection. Stateful inspection allows the firewall to track the state of active connections and make intelligent decisions based on the context of each connection.

To enable stateful inspection on a Cisco ASA firewall, you can use the following CLI command:

scssCopy code

ASA (config)# inspect [protocol]

Here, you specify the protocol you want to inspect (e.g., inspect tcp, inspect udp). Stateful inspection helps ensure that only valid, established connections are permitted while blocking unwanted or malicious traffic.

Intrusion detection and prevention systems (IDPS) integration is another advanced firewall technique. IDPS solutions complement traditional firewall rules by actively monitoring traffic for signs of suspicious or malicious activity and responding to threats in real-time.

To integrate an IDPS solution with a firewall, you can configure traffic redirection using CLI commands or the graphical user interface (GUI) provided by your firewall vendor. This redirection sends traffic to the IDPS for inspection before allowing or denying it based on the IDPS's findings.

In high-security environments, advanced firewall configurations often involve the use of network segmentation. Network segmentation divides a network into isolated segments or zones, each with its own set of firewall rules and security policies. This approach enhances security by containing breaches and limiting lateral movement for attackers.

To configure network segmentation, you can use firewall zones and inter-zone policies. For example, on a Palo Alto Networks firewall, you can define zones and create policies to control traffic between zones.

scssCopy code

PAN-OS (config)# set zone [zone-name] network [network-range] PAN-OS (config)# set policy from [source-zone] to [destination-zone] source [source-address] destination [destination-address] allow

By enforcing strict segmentation, you can minimize the attack surface and prevent unauthorized access between different parts of your network.

Firewall rules optimization is another crucial aspect of advanced firewall configuration. Over time, firewall rule sets can become complex and inefficient, impacting performance and manageability. Regularly reviewing and optimizing firewall rules ensures that the firewall operates at its peak performance and provides optimal security.

When optimizing firewall rules, consider using rule consolidation and reordering techniques. Consolidation involves combining similar rules to reduce the overall rule count, while reordering places the most commonly matched rules at the top of the rule set for faster processing.

Moreover, advanced firewall configurations often include the use of threat intelligence feeds. Threat intelligence feeds provide real-time information about known malicious IP addresses, domains, and indicators of compromise (IoCs). Integrating these feeds into your firewall allows you to automatically block traffic to and from known malicious sources.

To implement threat intelligence feeds in a firewall, you can use a threat intelligence platform or service that provides regular updates and indicators of malicious activity. Firewall vendors may offer built-in integration or APIs to connect with threat intelligence feeds.

Additionally, firewall rules can be enhanced with application-layer filtering and deep packet inspection (DPI). Application-layer filtering allows the firewall to identify and control traffic based on the specific applications or services being used, rather than just IP addresses and ports.

For instance, Palo Alto Networks firewalls offer Application ID and User ID features that enable granular control over application traffic. By understanding the applications within the traffic, the firewall can enforce policies based on application categories, such as social media, file sharing, or business applications.

Advanced firewall configurations may also involve the use of virtual firewalls or virtual security appliances (VSAs). Virtual firewalls operate within virtualized environments, providing security for virtual machines and cloud-based workloads.

To deploy a virtual firewall, you can use a hypervisor-specific deployment process, such as creating a virtual machine (VM) and installing the virtual firewall software. Many firewall vendors offer virtual versions of their products tailored for various virtualization platforms.

Furthermore, advanced firewall configurations often require the use of advanced threat detection and prevention techniques. These may include intrusion prevention systems (IPS), sandboxing, and behavioral analysis. These additional security layers can identify and mitigate zero-day threats and advanced malware that may evade traditional firewall rules.

To integrate an IPS solution with a firewall, you can set up a dedicated IPS device or use an integrated firewall-IPS appliance. Configuration may involve defining policies, signatures, and alerting thresholds to effectively detect and prevent intrusions.

Moreover, sandboxing solutions can be deployed alongside firewalls to analyze suspicious files and URLs in a controlled environment. Sandboxing helps identify and mitigate threats that exhibit unusual behavior or are not recognized by traditional signature-based defenses.

Behavioral analysis techniques, such as anomaly detection, can also be applied within the firewall to identify deviations from normal network behavior. By continuously monitoring network traffic and user activities, the firewall can raise alerts or take action when unusual patterns or activities are detected.

Furthermore, advanced firewall configurations often include high availability (HA) and failover mechanisms to ensure continuous protection. HA configurations involve deploying multiple firewall devices in an active-passive or active-active setup, where one firewall takes over if the primary firewall fails.

To configure HA and failover on firewalls, you can use vendor-specific CLI commands or GUI options. HA configurations may include synchronizing state information, virtual IP addresses, and ensuring rapid failover in case of hardware or software issues.

Lastly, advanced firewall configurations require robust logging and monitoring. Firewalls generate extensive logs that capture information about network traffic, rule matches, and security events. Centralized logging solutions and security information and event management (SIEM) platforms can be used to aggregate and analyze firewall logs. To configure firewall logging, you can specify log settings in the firewall's configuration, including log levels, destinations (e.g., syslog server), and log formats.

In summary, advanced firewall configuration involves a combination of techniques, strategies, and CLI commands to bolster network security. These include the use of ACLs, stateful inspection, intrusion detection and prevention, network segmentation, rule optimization, threat intelligence feeds, application-layer filtering, virtual firewalls, advanced threat detection, HA and failover mechanisms, and robust logging and monitoring. By implementing these advanced techniques, organizations can strengthen their defense against a wide range of cyber threats and ensure the integrity and availability of their networks.

Intrusion Detection Systems (IDS) are essential components of network security, serving as vigilant watchdogs that monitor network traffic and system behavior for signs of unauthorized or malicious activity. However, simply deploying an IDS is not sufficient; tuning and refining the system are equally critical to its effectiveness. Next, we will delve into the intricacies of IDS tuning, exploring techniques, strategies, and CLI commands to ensure that your IDS operates optimally and accurately detects threats.

To begin with, IDS tuning necessitates a comprehensive understanding of your network environment and the specific threats you want to detect. Conducting a thorough risk assessment is an essential first step. Identify critical assets, potential attack vectors, and the types of threats that pose the greatest risk to your organization. By understanding your network's unique characteristics and threat landscape, you can tailor your IDS tuning efforts effectively.

One key aspect of IDS tuning is defining a clear set of detection objectives. Determine the scope of the threats you intend to detect, whether they involve malware, network intrusions, insider threats, or other specific attack vectors. Once you have a precise detection scope, you can craft detection rules and policies that align with your objectives.

Intrusion detection rules play a central role in IDS tuning. These rules specify the conditions that trigger an alert when matched by network traffic or system events. Crafting effective rules requires a deep understanding of your network's normal behavior and the tactics, techniques, and procedures (TTPs) commonly employed by threat actors.

An example of a Snort IDS rule for detecting SQL injection attempts:

cssCopy code

```
alert tcp $EXTERNAL_NET any -> $SQL_SERVERS
$HTTP_PORTS (msg:"SQL Injection attempt";
flow:to_server,established; content:"' or '1'='1";
fast_pattern:only; nocase; http_uri; metadata:impact_flag
red, policy balanced-ips drop, service http;
reference:cve,CVE-2006-3392; classtype:web-application-
attack; sid:1234567; rev:1;)
```

This rule detects SQL injection attempts in HTTP traffic by looking for the specific payload "' or '1'='1". When a match occurs, it generates an alert.

Furthermore, IDS tuning often involves adjusting the sensitivity of detection rules. This sensitivity can be fine-tuned by modifying parameters like threshold values, match counts, or rate limits within rules. Tweaking these parameters allows you to strike a balance between reducing false positives and ensuring that legitimate threats are not missed.

For example, in Suricata, a network IDS/IPS, you can modify the threshold of a rule like this:

cssCopy code

```
alert tcp $EXTERNAL_NET any -> $HOME_NET $HTTP_PORTS
(msg:"HTTP request to a suspicious URL";
flow:established,to_server; content:"/suspicious-path/";
http_uri; threshold:type limit, track by_src, count 1,
seconds 60; sid:1234567;)
```

Here, the threshold is set to count a maximum of one occurrence of this rule per source IP address within a 60-second window. Adjusting the threshold values can help reduce noise.

Additionally, IDS tuning should involve rule optimization. Periodically review and revise your rules to remove obsolete or ineffective ones and add new rules to address emerging threats. Rule management is an ongoing process that requires constant vigilance and adaptation to the evolving threat landscape.

Intrusion detection systems often rely on signatures or patterns to identify known threats. Regularly updating these signatures is crucial for keeping your IDS effective. Subscription services or threat intelligence feeds provide up-to-date signatures for known threats, ensuring that your IDS can detect the latest malware variants and attack techniques.

For Snort, you can update the rule set using the following CLI command:

bashCopy code

```
sudo /usr/sbin/oinkmaster -C /etc/oinkmaster.conf -o /etc/snort/rules
```

This command updates Snort's rules based on the configuration specified in the oinkmaster.conf file.

Intrusion detection tuning also involves prioritizing alerts and incidents. Not all alerts are equally critical, and some may require immediate attention, while others can be investigated later. Implementing a severity or risk rating system allows you to categorize alerts and prioritize your response efforts effectively.

For example, you can assign different severity levels to Snort alerts using custom metadata:

cssCopy code

```
alert tcp $EXTERNAL_NET any -> $HTTP_SERVERS $HTTP_PORTS (msg:"Possible SQL Injection detected"; flow:to_server,established; content:"' or '1'='1"; nocase; http_uri; metadata:severity major; sid:1234567;)
```

Here, the metadata field assigns a "major" severity to the alert, indicating its higher priority.

Moreover, IDS tuning entails reducing false positives, which can overwhelm security teams and lead to alert fatigue. Fine-tuning rules and policies, as well as implementing whitelist and blacklist mechanisms, helps minimize false positives. Whitelists allow you to exclude trusted IP addresses or domains from triggering alerts, while blacklists block known malicious sources.

## Chapter 6: Quality of Service (QoS) Optimization

Traffic classification and marking are crucial aspects of network management and Quality of Service (QoS) implementation. These techniques help network administrators gain better control over network traffic, prioritize critical applications, and ensure efficient resource allocation. Next, we will explore the concepts of traffic classification and marking, along with the CLI commands and deployment strategies involved.

To begin with, traffic classification refers to the process of categorizing network traffic into different classes or categories based on specific criteria. This categorization allows network administrators to distinguish between various types of traffic, such as web browsing, VoIP, video streaming, and file downloads. By understanding the nature of each traffic type, administrators can apply appropriate QoS policies and optimizations to meet the network's performance and latency requirements.

One of the primary criteria used for traffic classification is the source and destination IP addresses. Administrators can define access control lists (ACLs) or prefix lists to identify traffic flows between specific IP addresses or subnets. For instance, Cisco devices support the use of ACLs for traffic classification, and the following CLI command demonstrates how to create an ACL:

Copy code

access-list 100 permit ip source_ip destination_ip

In this command, "access-list 100" defines an ACL with a permit statement for traffic between the specified source and destination IP addresses. This is a basic example of traffic classification based on IP addresses.

Another criterion for traffic classification is the type of application or protocol being used. Deep Packet Inspection (DPI) and Application Layer Gateway (ALG) technologies are commonly employed to identify and classify traffic based on the application layer data. DPI examines packet payloads to recognize specific application signatures, while ALGs are designed to work with well-known application protocols.

For example, a firewall or security appliance can use DPI to identify and classify traffic patterns associated with popular applications like Skype or BitTorrent. Once identified, administrators can apply policies to control or prioritize this traffic accordingly.

In addition to IP addresses and application signatures, traffic classification can also consider Layer 4 port numbers. Different applications and services typically use specific port numbers, making it possible to classify traffic based on port ranges. Network administrators can configure traffic classifiers to recognize traffic associated with common ports, such as port 80 for HTTP or port 443 for HTTPS.

Here's an example of a Cisco CLI command to classify traffic based on port numbers using a class map:

pythonCopy code

```
class-map match-all HTTP-Traffic match access-group 101
! access-list 101 permit tcp any any eq 80
```

In this example, a class map named "HTTP-Traffic" is defined to match traffic specified by access-list 101, which permits TCP traffic on port 80 (HTTP).

Once traffic has been classified, the next step is marking or tagging packets to indicate their respective classes. Traffic marking typically involves setting the Differentiated Services Code Point (DSCP) field in the IP header or the 802.1p priority field in the Ethernet header. These markings provide a way for routers and switches to prioritize and manage traffic based on their class.

To mark traffic, administrators can use policies and configurations on network devices. For instance, Cisco devices support the use of policy maps and class maps to mark traffic based on the classification. Here's an example of marking traffic with a specific DSCP value using Cisco's Modular QoS CLI (MQC):

arduinoCopy code

```
policy-map Mark-Traffic class  HTTP-Traffic set dscp af21
```

In this example, a policy map named "Mark-Traffic" is defined, and it includes a class called "HTTP-Traffic," which is configured to set the DSCP value to af21 for packets matching this class.

Marked traffic can then be subjected to various QoS treatments, such as bandwidth allocation, queue prioritization, or traffic shaping. These treatments ensure that high-priority traffic receives preferential treatment over lower-priority traffic, optimizing network performance and user experience.

In summary, traffic classification and marking are essential techniques for effective network management and QoS implementation. By categorizing and tagging traffic based on specific criteria, administrators can shape, prioritize, and control network traffic to meet their organization's performance and latency requirements. Understanding the CLI commands and deployment strategies for traffic classification and marking is vital for network administrators seeking to optimize their networks.

Advanced Quality of Service (QoS) policies are an integral part of modern network management, enabling organizations to prioritize, control, and optimize the flow of traffic within their networks. Next, we delve into the concepts, strategies, and techniques for deploying advanced QoS policies.

QoS policies go beyond the basic classification and marking of network traffic. They involve more intricate methods for managing bandwidth, reducing latency, and ensuring the performance of critical applications. These advanced policies allow network administrators to tailor the network to meet specific business requirements and provide a superior user experience.

One common approach to advanced QoS is the use of traffic shaping and traffic policing. Traffic shaping is a technique that smooths the traffic flow by buffering packets during congestion and then releasing them at a controlled rate. This helps prevent network congestion and minimizes packet loss. To deploy traffic shaping, administrators can configure shaping parameters on routers or switches using the Command Line Interface (CLI). For instance, Cisco routers support the use of the "shape" command:

kotlinCopy code

```
interface GigabitEthernet0/0 shape average 10000000 //
Shapes traffic to an average of 10 Mbps
```

In this example, traffic shaping is applied to the GigabitEthernet0/0 interface to limit the outbound traffic rate to an average of 10 Mbps.

Traffic policing, on the other hand, involves monitoring traffic and taking action when it exceeds specified rate limits. This method can be used to drop or remark packets that exceed predefined thresholds. Cisco routers provide a "police" command for traffic policing:

kotlinCopy code

```
interface GigabitEthernet0/0 police 5000000 100000
exceed-action drop // Polices traffic to 5 Mbps with a burst
rate of 100 Kbps
```

In this command, traffic policing is applied to limit traffic on the GigabitEthernet0/0 interface to 5 Mbps, with a burst rate of 100 Kbps.

Another advanced QoS technique is the use of Hierarchical QoS (HQoS) or Multi-Level QoS. HQoS allows network administrators to define multiple levels of QoS policies, each with its own classification, marking, and policing rules. This hierarchical approach provides finer control over how different classes of traffic are treated within the network.

To implement HQoS, administrators can configure class maps and policy maps at various levels in the hierarchy. For example, they can define a top-level policy map for overall bandwidth allocation and then create nested policy maps for specific traffic classes within that top-level policy. This allows for granular control and efficient resource allocation.

In addition to shaping and policing, advanced QoS policies often involve the use of traffic queuing and prioritization mechanisms. Weighted Fair Queuing (WFQ), Class-Based Weighted Fair Queuing (CBWFQ), and Low Latency Queuing (LLQ) are common queuing methods that ensure fair distribution of bandwidth among different traffic classes. These queuing techniques can be configured using CLI commands on network devices.

For instance, Cisco routers support LLQ for low-latency traffic prioritization:

kotlinCopy code

```
policy-map LLQ-Policy class LLQ-Traffic priority percent 30
class Bulk-Traffic bandwidth percent 70
```

In this example, LLQ is applied to prioritize LLQ-Traffic by allocating 30% of the available bandwidth to this class, while the remaining 70% is allocated to Bulk-Traffic.

Advanced QoS policies can also include the use of QoS pre-classify, which is essential when dealing with encrypted traffic, such as IPsec VPNs. QoS pre-classify allows network devices to inspect and classify traffic based on its inner, unencrypted headers before encryption occurs. This ensures that QoS policies are applied accurately to the traffic.

To deploy QoS pre-classify on a Cisco device, administrators can use the following CLI command:

arduinoCopy code

```
crypto ipsec df-bit clear-df
```

This command enables the device to clear the Don't Fragment (DF) bit from the inner IP header, allowing it to inspect and classify the traffic before encryption.

Advanced QoS policies also encompass strategies for managing bursty traffic, ensuring low latency for real-time applications, and optimizing WAN links for efficient data transfer. These techniques may involve the use of shaping, queuing, and rate limiting to meet specific performance requirements.

In summary, advanced QoS policies are a vital component of network management, enabling organizations to optimize their network performance, prioritize critical applications, and provide a superior user experience. By employing techniques like traffic shaping, traffic policing, hierarchical QoS, queuing mechanisms, and QoS pre-classify, network administrators can fine-tune their networks to meet the specific needs of their businesses. Understanding the CLI commands and deployment strategies for these advanced QoS policies is essential for effective network management and optimization.

**Chapter 7: Scalability and High Availability Strategies**

Load balancing and clustering techniques are essential components of modern network infrastructure, providing enhanced performance, scalability, and fault tolerance. Next, we explore the concepts, strategies, and deployment methods for load balancing and clustering in network environments.

Load balancing is the process of distributing network traffic across multiple servers or resources to optimize resource utilization and ensure high availability. It is commonly used in data centers, web services, and applications to evenly distribute incoming requests and prevent individual servers from becoming overwhelmed.

One of the most widely used load balancing techniques is Round Robin DNS (Domain Name System). This method involves configuring multiple IP addresses for a single domain name, with each IP pointing to a different server. When a client requests the domain, the DNS server responds with one of the IP addresses in a cyclic manner, effectively distributing traffic among the servers.

To deploy Round Robin DNS, administrators need to create DNS records for each server and configure the DNS server accordingly. No additional CLI commands are necessary for this technique.

Another load balancing approach is to use a dedicated load balancer device or software, such as HAProxy or Nginx. These load balancers distribute traffic based on predefined rules, ensuring that each server receives a fair share of requests. The configuration of load balancer software typically involves editing configuration files or using a web-based interface, depending on the chosen software.

For instance, when configuring HAProxy, administrators can create a backend section in the configuration file to define the servers to be load balanced:

sqlCopy code

```
backend my-backend balance roundrobin server server1
192.168.1.100:80 check server server2 192.168.1.101:80
check
```

In this example, HAProxy is configured to balance traffic between server1 and server2, both listening on port 80. The "check" keyword indicates that HAProxy should monitor the health of these servers.

In addition to traditional load balancing, Content Delivery Networks (CDNs) are widely used to distribute content and optimize the delivery of web applications. CDNs cache content on multiple servers distributed across different geographical locations. When a user requests content, the CDN automatically routes the request to the nearest server with the cached content, reducing latency and improving load times.

To implement a CDN, organizations typically subscribe to CDN services from providers like Akamai, Cloudflare, or Amazon CloudFront. The configuration process typically involves signing up for the service, configuring DNS settings, and adjusting caching policies through the provider's web-based dashboard.

Clustering, on the other hand, involves grouping multiple servers or nodes into a single entity to work together as a cohesive unit. Clusters are often used to enhance fault tolerance, scalability, and performance of services and applications.

One popular clustering technique is the use of Network Load Balancers (NLB) in conjunction with clusters of servers. NLB distributes incoming traffic to a cluster of servers based on load balancing algorithms and ensures that traffic is redirected to healthy nodes. Deploying NLB involves configuring it on a Windows Server environment using PowerShell commands.

For instance, administrators can use PowerShell to install the NLB feature:

mathematicaCopy code

```
Install-WindowsFeature -Name NLB
```

After installation, they can configure NLB for a specific cluster:

sqlCopy code

```
New-NlbCluster -InterfaceName "Ethernet" -ClusterName "MyCluster" -OperationMode Unicast
```

In this example, NLB is configured with the name "MyCluster" and set to operate in Unicast mode.

Another clustering technique is the creation of High Availability (HA) clusters using software like Microsoft Failover Clustering or Linux High Availability (HA). These clusters ensure that services and applications remain available even if individual servers fail.

To deploy an HA cluster in a Windows Server environment, administrators can use PowerShell commands to create and configure the cluster:

sqlCopy code

```
New-Cluster -Name "MyCluster" -Node "Server1", "Server2" -StaticAddress "192.168.1.10"
```

In this command, a new cluster named "MyCluster" is created with two nodes (Server1 and Server2) and a static IP address of 192.168.1.10.

For Linux-based environments, administrators can use the Pacemaker and Corosync software to configure HA clusters. This involves editing cluster configuration files and running commands to start and manage the cluster.

In summary, load balancing and clustering techniques are crucial for optimizing network performance, ensuring high availability, and enhancing scalability. These techniques distribute network traffic or workload across multiple resources, preventing bottlenecks and providing fault tolerance. Whether deploying Round Robin DNS, using dedicated load balancers, or setting up clusters with NLB or HA clustering software, administrators must have a solid understanding of the chosen techniques and the corresponding CLI commands or configuration methods to implement them effectively.

Redundancy and failover solutions are fundamental components of network design, ensuring that critical systems remain available even in the face of hardware failures or unexpected outages. Next, we will explore the concepts, strategies, and deployment methods for redundancy and failover in network environments.

Redundancy is the practice of duplicating critical components or systems within a network to provide backup resources that can seamlessly take over in case of a failure. One common use case for redundancy is in the design of mission-critical services such as web servers, database servers, and network switches.

One method of achieving redundancy is through the use of Network Load Balancers (NLBs). NLBs distribute incoming traffic across multiple servers, ensuring that if one server fails, the others can continue to handle the load. The configuration of NLBs typically involves using command-line tools or a web-based interface, depending on the specific implementation.

For instance, when setting up a Network Load Balancer in an Amazon Web Services (AWS) environment, administrators can use the AWS Command Line Interface (CLI) to create and configure the NLB:

cssCopy code

aws elbv2 create-load-balancer --name my-load-balancer -- subnets subnet-12345678 subnet-87654321 --security- groups sg-0123456789 abcdef0

In this example, an NLB named "my-load-balancer" is created, specifying the subnets and security groups.

Another form of redundancy is server clustering, where multiple servers work together as a single entity, with one server taking over if another fails. Clustering is often used for services like file sharing, databases, and virtualization.

For instance, Microsoft Windows Server offers Failover Clustering, which allows administrators to create a cluster of servers that provide high availability for services and applications. The configuration of a Windows Failover Cluster can be achieved through the Failover Cluster Manager GUI or by using PowerShell commands:

sqlCopy code

New-Cluster -Name MyCluster -Node Node1, Node2 - StaticAddress 192.168.1.10

In this command, a new cluster named "MyCluster" is created with two nodes (Node1 and Node2) and a static IP address of 192.168.1.10.

Redundancy can also be implemented at the network level through technologies like Virtual Router Redundancy Protocol (VRRP) or Hot Standby Router Protocol (HSRP). These protocols enable multiple routers to work together as a single virtual router, with one router actively processing traffic and the others standing by as backups.

To configure VRRP on a Cisco router, administrators can use CLI commands. For example:

kotlinCopy code

```
interface GigabitEthernet0/0 ip address 192.168.1.1
255.255.255.0 standby 1 ip 192.168.1.254 standby 1
priority 110 standby 1 preempt
```

In this configuration, the router is assigned an IP address of
192.168.1.1, and VRRP is configured with a virtual IP of
192.168.1.254. The "priority" setting determines the active
router, and "preempt" ensures that the router with the
highest priority becomes the active one.

Failover solutions, on the other hand, are mechanisms that
automatically switch from a primary system to a secondary
system when the primary experiences a failure. These
solutions are commonly used for internet connectivity,
where maintaining a continuous connection is essential.

One example of a failover solution is the use of multiple
internet service providers (ISPs) with Border Gateway
Protocol (BGP) routing. BGP allows organizations to
advertise their IP prefixes through multiple ISPs. If one ISP
experiences an outage, BGP will automatically reroute traffic
through the remaining active ISP.

The deployment of BGP involves configuring BGP routers and
peering with multiple ISPs. CLI commands are used
extensively in this process, including the configuration of
BGP neighbors and route advertisements.

perlCopy code

```
router bgp 65000 neighbor 203.0.113.1 remote-as 65500
neighbor 203.0.113.1 description ISP1 neighbor
203.0.113.2 remote-as 65501 neighbor 203.0.113.2
description ISP2 ! ip prefix-list my-prefix permit
192.0.2.0/24 ! route-map my-route-map permit 10
match ip address prefix-list my-prefix set local-preference
200 ! router bgp 65000 address-family ipv4 neighbor
203.0.113.1 activate neighbor 203.0.113.1 route-map
```

my-route-map in neighbor 203.0.113.2 activate neighbor 203.0.113.2 route-map my-route-map in exit-address-family

In this BGP configuration, the router is set up to peer with two ISPs (ISP1 and ISP2), and a route-map is used to manipulate routing preferences.

Additionally, software-defined networking (SDN) technologies, such as Software-Defined Wide Area Network (SD-WAN), provide intelligent failover solutions. SD-WAN solutions can automatically reroute traffic through alternative paths, including backup internet links or private networks, when connectivity issues are detected.

To implement SD-WAN, organizations need to select an SD-WAN solution, configure their SD-WAN devices, and establish policies for failover and traffic prioritization. While specific CLI commands may vary depending on the chosen SD-WAN vendor, the process generally involves command-line configuration of SD-WAN routers and controllers.

In summary, redundancy and failover solutions are essential for ensuring high availability and fault tolerance in network environments. Whether implementing redundancy through load balancers, server clustering, or network protocols like VRRP, or deploying failover solutions like BGP routing or SD-WAN, network administrators must have a solid understanding of the chosen techniques and the corresponding CLI commands or configuration methods to achieve robust and reliable network designs.

**Chapter 8: Cloud Integration and Hybrid Networks**

Cloud service integration has become a critical aspect of modern IT infrastructure, enabling organizations to harness the power and flexibility of cloud computing resources to meet their business needs. Next, we will delve into the best practices for effectively integrating cloud services into your existing infrastructure, addressing various deployment scenarios and potential challenges along the way.

One fundamental aspect of cloud service integration is selecting the appropriate cloud service provider that aligns with your organization's goals and requirements. Major cloud providers like Amazon Web Services (AWS), Microsoft Azure, and Google Cloud Platform (GCP) offer a wide range of services and features. The choice should be made based on factors such as service offerings, pricing models, data residency requirements, and compliance considerations.

For instance, AWS provides a vast array of services, including computing, storage, databases, machine learning, and more. Organizations can leverage the AWS Management Console, a web-based interface, or AWS Command Line Interface (CLI) to provision and manage resources. To create an AWS Elastic Compute Cloud (EC2) instance using CLI, you can use the following command:

```css
cssCopy code
aws ec2 run-instances --image-id ami-0123456789abcdef0 --instance-type t2.micro --key-name MyKeyPair --subnet-id subnet-0123456789abcdef0
```

In this command, a t2.micro EC2 instance is launched using a specified Amazon Machine Image (AMI) and a key pair for secure SSH access.

Once the cloud provider is chosen, organizations should consider integrating cloud services seamlessly with their existing on-premises infrastructure. Hybrid cloud architectures, which combine on-premises data centers and public or private cloud resources, are common in many enterprises. Proper network connectivity and security measures are crucial to ensure efficient data flow between these environments.

Virtual Private Networks (VPNs) or dedicated connections, such as AWS Direct Connect or Azure ExpressRoute, can establish secure communication channels between on-premises networks and cloud resources. VPN configuration varies depending on the cloud provider and the on-premises network devices. In AWS, for instance, setting up a VPN connection might involve configuring a Virtual Private Gateway, Customer Gateway, and VPN connection through the AWS Management Console or CLI.

cssCopy code

```
aws ec2 create-vpn-connection --customer-gateway-id cgw-0123456789abcdef0 --type ipsec.1 --options "{\"StaticRoutesOnly\":true}" --vpn-gateway-id vgw-0123456789abcdef0 --transit-gateway-id tgw-0123456789abcdef0 --tag-specifications "ResourceType=vpn-connection,Tags=[{Key=Name,Value=MyVPNConnection}]"
```

This CLI command creates an AWS VPN connection between a Customer Gateway and a Virtual Private Gateway.

Cloud services often require proper identity and access management (IAM) to ensure that only authorized personnel can access resources. Cloud providers offer IAM services that allow organizations to define roles, permissions, and access policies.

In AWS, the Identity and Access Management (IAM) service can be managed using CLI commands. To create an IAM user, you can use a command like this:

sqlCopy code

```
aws iam create-user --user-name MyIAMUser
```

Once the user is created, access policies and permissions can be attached to the user to grant or restrict access to specific AWS services and resources.

Data integration is a critical aspect of cloud service integration. Organizations must consider data migration, synchronization, and backup strategies when moving data to and from the cloud. Cloud storage services like Amazon S3, Azure Blob Storage, and Google Cloud Storage provide scalable and durable storage solutions.

To copy files to an Amazon S3 bucket using the AWS CLI, you can use the "aws s3 cp" command:

bashCopy code

```
aws s3 cp my-file.txt s3://my-bucket/
```

This command uploads "my-file.txt" to the specified S3 bucket.

Data encryption and compliance are also vital aspects of data integration. Organizations should encrypt sensitive data both in transit and at rest. Cloud providers offer encryption services and tools to help organizations secure their data effectively.

Ensuring high availability and fault tolerance in a cloud environment involves designing redundant architectures, utilizing load balancers, and implementing autoscaling. Load balancers distribute incoming traffic across multiple instances, ensuring that applications remain accessible even if some instances fail.

In AWS, the Elastic Load Balancer (ELB) service provides load balancing capabilities. To create an Application Load

Balancer (ALB) using CLI commands, you can use the following:

cssCopy code

```
aws elbv2 create-load-balancer --name MyLoadBalancer --subnets subnet-0123456789abcdef0 subnet-876543210fedcba9 --security-groups sg-0123456789abcdef0
```

This command creates an ALB named "MyLoadBalancer" in specified subnets and security groups.

For high availability, organizations should consider deploying resources across multiple availability zones or regions provided by cloud providers. In AWS, this can be achieved by selecting the appropriate availability zones when launching instances or deploying resources.

Cost management is another essential consideration in cloud service integration. Organizations should continuously monitor their cloud usage, implement cost allocation tags, and optimize resources to avoid unexpected expenses. Cloud providers offer billing and cost management tools to help organizations track and manage their cloud spending.

Cloud service integration best practices also include disaster recovery planning. Organizations should regularly back up data and implement disaster recovery solutions to minimize downtime and data loss in case of unforeseen events. Cloud providers offer services like AWS Backup or Azure Site Recovery to facilitate disaster recovery planning and execution.

Security is paramount in cloud service integration. Organizations should follow industry best practices for securing cloud resources, including regular security assessments, patch management, and vulnerability scanning. Many cloud providers offer security and compliance tools to help organizations enhance their security posture.

Additionally, organizations should implement monitoring and alerting solutions to detect and respond to security incidents promptly. Cloud providers offer monitoring services, such as Amazon CloudWatch or Azure Monitor, which can be configured to send alerts based on predefined conditions or thresholds.

In summary, cloud service integration best practices encompass various aspects, including cloud provider selection, network connectivity, IAM, data integration, security, cost management, disaster recovery, and monitoring. Organizations should carefully plan and execute their cloud integration strategies to harness the full benefits of cloud computing while ensuring the security, reliability, and cost-effectiveness of their IT operations.

Hybrid network connectivity, the integration of both on-premises and cloud resources, is becoming increasingly popular among organizations looking to balance the advantages of traditional infrastructure with the flexibility and scalability offered by cloud computing. Next, we will explore the various hybrid network connectivity options available, including methods to seamlessly connect on-premises data centers to cloud environments.

One of the most common approaches to hybrid network connectivity is through the use of virtual private networks (VPNs). VPNs establish secure, encrypted connections over public networks like the internet, allowing remote sites or users to connect to a corporate network or cloud resources.

For example, organizations can leverage AWS Direct Connect, which provides dedicated, high-speed network connections between on-premises data centers and AWS cloud resources. To configure AWS Direct Connect using the AWS Command Line Interface (CLI), organizations can follow these steps:

Set up a Direct Connect Gateway using the **create-direct-connect-gateway** command.

Create a virtual interface with the **create-private-virtual-interface** or **create-public-virtual-interface** command.

Configure your on-premises routers and establish a connection to the AWS Direct Connect location.

By following these CLI commands, organizations can establish a dedicated, private connection to AWS resources, ensuring low-latency, high-bandwidth access.

Another hybrid network connectivity option is the use of cloud interconnects, which provide direct connections to cloud providers via service providers or colocation data centers. These interconnects offer higher bandwidth and lower latency than traditional internet connections.

For instance, Microsoft Azure ExpressRoute allows organizations to connect their on-premises data centers to Azure via private, dedicated connections provided by Azure ExpressRoute partners. To create an ExpressRoute circuit using the Azure CLI, you can use the following steps:

Create an ExpressRoute circuit with the **az network express-route circuit create** command.

Define the peering settings and authorization key.

Configure your on-premises routers to establish a connection with the Azure ExpressRoute location.

By executing these CLI commands, organizations can establish a dedicated, high-speed connection to Azure, bypassing the public internet.

Hybrid cloud scenarios often involve the use of Software-Defined Wide Area Network (SD-WAN) solutions, which optimize and manage traffic between on-premises and cloud resources. SD-WAN solutions enhance network performance, improve application delivery, and provide centralized management and control.

For instance, Cisco's SD-WAN solution can be configured using the Cisco vManage Controller. To create and manage SD-WAN policies, administrators can use the vManage CLI: Access the vManage CLI via SSH or console.

Use the **configure** command to enter configuration mode.

Define SD-WAN policies, including application optimization, traffic steering, and QoS settings.

Apply policies to specific network interfaces and devices.

These CLI commands enable organizations to fine-tune their SD-WAN configurations for optimal hybrid network connectivity.

Additionally, organizations can employ hybrid cloud gateways, which serve as intermediaries between on-premises networks and cloud environments. These gateways provide secure, controlled access to cloud resources while simplifying network management.

For example, the Google Cloud Interconnect Partner Program allows organizations to connect to Google Cloud Platform (GCP) resources via partner networks. To configure a dedicated interconnect connection with GCP, organizations can use the GCP Console or Google Cloud CLI:

Create a dedicated interconnect connection using the **gcloud compute interconnects create** command.

Specify the interconnect details, such as location, VLAN attachment, and bandwidth.

Establish physical connectivity with GCP at the chosen colocation facility.

By executing these CLI commands, organizations can establish dedicated, high-speed connections to GCP resources through approved interconnect partners.

Hybrid network connectivity options also extend to the realm of multicloud, allowing organizations to connect and manage resources across multiple cloud providers.

Multicloud solutions offer redundancy, flexibility, and the ability to leverage the strengths of different cloud platforms. One approach to multicloud connectivity is through the use of cloud-native network services provided by individual cloud providers. For instance, AWS Transit Gateway and Azure Virtual WAN offer multicloud networking capabilities that allow organizations to connect VPCs, VNets, and on-premises networks seamlessly.

To set up AWS Transit Gateway, organizations can use the AWS CLI:

Create a Transit Gateway using the **create-transit-gateway** command.

Attach VPCs and VPN connections to the Transit Gateway.

Configure route tables and route propagation to enable communication between connected networks.

By following these CLI commands, organizations can establish a multicloud network architecture in AWS.

Similarly, Azure Virtual WAN enables multicloud connectivity using the Azure CLI:

Create a Virtual WAN with the **az network vpn-site create** command.

Configure VPN sites and connections to Azure, AWS, or other networks.

Define routing preferences and policies to control traffic flow.

By executing these CLI commands, organizations can implement multicloud connectivity in Azure, allowing them to connect to multiple cloud providers simultaneously.

## Chapter 9: Network Automation and DevOps Practices

Automation tools and scripting have become indispensable in modern network management and operations, empowering organizations to streamline repetitive tasks, enhance efficiency, and reduce human errors. Next, we delve into the world of automation tools and scripting, exploring their significance, deployment techniques, and the benefits they offer to network professionals.

Network automation is a paradigm shift in how networks are configured, managed, and maintained. It involves the use of software and scripts to perform tasks traditionally carried out manually. By automating network operations, organizations can respond rapidly to changing demands, reduce operational costs, and enhance network agility.

One of the fundamental tools used in network automation is the Command Line Interface (CLI). CLI-based automation allows network engineers to write scripts that interact with network devices using command-line commands. For example, to automate the process of backing up router configurations, one can create a simple Bash script that uses SSH and CLI commands:

```bash
bashCopy code
#!/bin/bash        # Define device parameters
device_ip="192.168.1.1"        device_username="admin"
device_password="password"   # Establish an SSH
connection ssh $device_username@$device_ip  <<  EOF
terminal length 0 show running-config exit EOF
```

This script connects to a network device using SSH, sets the terminal length to 0 to retrieve the entire configuration, and then displays it. The configuration can be saved to a file for backup purposes.

Another powerful automation tool is Ansible, an open-source automation platform that simplifies complex network tasks. Ansible uses a declarative language to define the desired state of network devices, making it easier to automate configurations and enforce consistency.

To automate network device configurations with Ansible, one typically creates YAML playbooks that describe the desired configurations. For example, to configure VLANs on multiple switches, an Ansible playbook may look like this:

yamlCopy code

```
--- - hosts: switches tasks: - name: Configure VLANs
ios_vlan: vlan_id: "{{ item.id }}" name: "{{ item.name }}"
state: present with_items: - { id: 10, name: "Sales" } - {
id: 20, name: "Engineering" }
```

This playbook instructs Ansible to configure VLANs with specific IDs and names on a group of network switches. Ansible then connects to each switch and applies the configurations.

Another prevalent automation tool is Puppet, which focuses on configuration management. Puppet allows organizations to define the desired state of network devices and automatically enforce those states. Puppet manifests, written in Puppet's domain-specific language (DSL), describe configurations and dependencies.

To automate the installation and configuration of software packages on network devices using Puppet, one can create a manifest like this:

puppetCopy code

```
package { 'httpd': ensure => 'installed', } service { 'httpd':
ensure => 'running', enable => true, }
```

This Puppet manifest ensures that the Apache web server package is installed and the service is running on the target network device.

Python, a versatile and widely used programming language, is a scripting powerhouse for network automation. Python's extensive libraries and frameworks, such as Paramiko and Netmiko, facilitate network automation tasks like device configuration, monitoring, and data retrieval.

For instance, to automate the retrieval of interface statistics from network switches using Python and the Netmiko library, one can write a script like this:

pythonCopy code

```
from netmiko import ConnectHandler # Define device parameters device = { 'device_type': 'cisco_ios', 'ip': '192.168.1.1', 'username': 'admin', 'password': 'password', } # Connect to the device connection = ConnectHandler(**device) # Execute a show command output = connection.send_command('show interface GigabitEthernet1/0/1') # Print the command output print(output) # Close the connection connection.disconnect()
```

This Python script connects to a network switch, executes a show command to retrieve interface statistics, and prints the output.

Ansible, Puppet, and Python are just a few examples of the automation tools and scripting languages available to network professionals. The choice of tool or language depends on factors like organizational preferences, existing infrastructure, and specific automation needs.

Automation brings a myriad of benefits to network management. It accelerates provisioning and deployment, reduces errors, enhances network consistency, and frees up valuable human resources for more strategic tasks. With automation, organizations can achieve agility, scalability, and operational efficiency in their network environments.

In addition to the tools and languages mentioned, infrastructure-as-code (IaC) is gaining traction as a methodology for managing network resources through code. IaC allows organizations to define and deploy network configurations using code, treating infrastructure elements as programmable resources.

Terraform, a popular IaC tool, enables the provisioning of network infrastructure on various cloud platforms. A Terraform configuration file, written in HashiCorp Configuration Language (HCL), describes the desired infrastructure state.

To create a virtual private cloud (VPC) on AWS using Terraform, one can create a configuration like this:

hclCopy code

```
provider "aws" { region = "us-east-1" } resource "aws_vpc" "example" { cidr_block = "10.0.0.0/16" } resource "aws_subnet" "example" { vpc_id = aws_vpc.example.id cidr_block = "10.0.1.0/24" } resource "aws_security_group" "example" { name = "example" description = "Example security group" } # Other resource configurations (e.g., instances, load balancers) can be added here.
```

This Terraform configuration defines an AWS VPC, subnet, and security group, allowing organizations to provision network infrastructure programmatically.

As organizations embrace automation, they often adopt version control systems like Git to manage automation scripts and configurations. Git enables collaboration, version tracking, and rollback capabilities, enhancing the reliability of automated tasks.

To manage automation scripts with Git, one can follow these steps:

Initialize a Git repository in the project directory using the **git init** command.

Add automation scripts and configuration files to the repository using **git add**.

Commit changes with a descriptive message using **git commit**.

Push the repository to a Git hosting service like GitHub or GitLab.

Version control ensures that automation scripts are maintained, tracked, and easily recoverable in case of errors or changes.

In summary, automation tools and scripting are integral to modern network management, offering network professionals the means to streamline operations, reduce manual tasks, and enhance efficiency. Whether using CLI scripting, Ansible, Puppet, Python, or infrastructure-as-code tools like Terraform, organizations can reap the benefits of automation, enabling agility and scalability in their network environments. Moreover, the adoption of version control systems like Git ensures the reliability and maintainability of automation scripts and configurations. As technology continues to evolve, network automation will remain a pivotal aspect of network management and operations.

Infrastructure as Code (IaC) and DevOps workflows represent a transformative approach to managing and deploying IT infrastructure, ushering in a new era of efficiency, collaboration, and scalability in the world of technology.

IaC, at its core, is a practice that treats infrastructure configurations as code, allowing IT professionals to automate the provisioning and management of resources through code and scripts. This approach offers numerous advantages, such as repeatability, consistency, and scalability, making it a fundamental element of modern IT operations.

One of the key elements of IaC is the use of version control systems like Git, which enable teams to collaboratively work on infrastructure code, track changes, and maintain a historical record of configurations. Git facilitates the management of infrastructure code just as it does with software code, allowing for rollbacks, branching, and merging.

In a typical IaC workflow, infrastructure code is written using domain-specific languages like HashiCorp Configuration Language (HCL) for tools like Terraform or YAML for tools like Ansible. These declarative languages describe the desired state of infrastructure resources, such as servers, networks, and storage.

For instance, to define an AWS EC2 instance using Terraform, one would write a configuration like this:

hclCopy code

```
resource "aws_instance" "example" { ami = "ami-0c55b159cbfafe1f0" instance_type = "t2.micro" }
```

This Terraform code defines an EC2 instance with a specific Amazon Machine Image (AMI) and instance type. When applied, Terraform will automatically provision the instance with the desired configuration.

In addition to Terraform, tools like Ansible provide a powerful platform for IaC. Ansible playbooks, written in YAML, describe infrastructure configurations and the tasks needed to achieve the desired state. Here's an example Ansible playbook that installs and configures Nginx on multiple servers:

yamlCopy code

```
--- - hosts: web_servers tasks: - name: Install Nginx apt:
name: nginx state: present - name: Start Nginx service
service: name: nginx state: started
```

This Ansible playbook specifies that Nginx should be installed
and the service started on a group of servers designated as
"web_servers."

DevOps, on the other hand, is a cultural and organizational
philosophy that emphasizes collaboration between
development and operations teams. It aims to shorten the
software development lifecycle, increase the frequency of
releases, and improve the quality and reliability of software
and infrastructure.

IaC and DevOps are deeply interconnected. IaC provides the
technical foundation for implementing DevOps practices,
enabling the automation of infrastructure provisioning,
configuration management, and application deployment.
This automation is critical for achieving the goals of DevOps,
such as continuous integration, continuous delivery, and
continuous monitoring.

A typical DevOps workflow incorporates several key
practices and tools. Continuous Integration (CI) involves the
automatic building, testing, and integration of code changes
into a shared repository. CI tools like Jenkins, Travis CI, or
CircleCI can be configured to trigger automated tests and
deployments whenever code changes are pushed to a
version control repository.

For example, a CI pipeline for a web application might
involve running unit tests, conducting code quality checks,
and deploying the application to a staging environment. CLI
commands used in this process might include running test
suites or executing deployment scripts.

Continuous Delivery (CD) takes the CI process a step further
by automating the deployment of code changes to
production or production-like environments. CD pipelines

are designed to ensure that code changes are consistently and safely deployed to various stages of the application lifecycle, from development and testing to staging and production.

A typical CD pipeline might involve the use of configuration files that define the deployment process and CLI commands to deploy the application to different environments. For instance, a deployment script might use CLI commands like **docker-compose up** to deploy a containerized application.

Infrastructure as Code plays a pivotal role in enabling CD by automating the provisioning and configuration of infrastructure components, ensuring that infrastructure evolves in tandem with code changes.

The DevOps philosophy also emphasizes monitoring and feedback as critical components of the software development lifecycle. Continuous Monitoring involves the use of tools and practices to collect, analyze, and visualize data from application and infrastructure components. These insights enable teams to detect issues early, optimize performance, and make data-driven decisions.

CLI commands for monitoring often involve querying logs, metrics, or events generated by various components of the infrastructure and application stack. For example, the **grep** command can be used to search for specific log entries, while the **curl** command can fetch data from APIs for monitoring purposes.

Automation is a central tenet of DevOps workflows, and both IaC and CI/CD pipelines rely heavily on scripting and CLI commands to automate tasks, orchestrate processes, and enforce policies. These scripts and commands are typically executed within automation servers or containers, ensuring consistency and repeatability in the deployment and management of infrastructure and applications.

As DevOps practices continue to evolve, tools and techniques for IaC and automation are constantly improving. New tools, such as Kubernetes for container orchestration and Helm for package management, are becoming essential components of DevOps toolchains, allowing for more streamlined and efficient deployment and scaling of applications.

In summary, Infrastructure as Code and DevOps workflows represent a dynamic and interconnected approach to managing and deploying IT infrastructure and applications. IaC provides the foundation for automating infrastructure provisioning and configuration, while DevOps practices enable collaboration, automation, and continuous improvement across development and operations teams. CLI commands and scripting play a pivotal role in both IaC and DevOps, enabling the automation of tasks, deployment processes, and monitoring, ultimately leading to increased agility, reliability, and efficiency in modern IT operations.

## Chapter 10: Case Studies in Complex Troubleshooting

Complex network outage resolution is a challenging but critical aspect of network management and operations, requiring a systematic and strategic approach to diagnose and resolve issues efficiently and effectively. During a network outage, organizations can experience significant disruptions, resulting in downtime, loss of productivity, and potentially severe financial consequences. Therefore, having a well-defined methodology for handling complex network outages is essential.

The first step in resolving a complex network outage is to establish clear incident ownership and communication channels. This ensures that the right people are aware of the issue and can collaborate to address it promptly. Incident ownership typically falls on a network engineer or administrator responsible for the affected infrastructure.

Once ownership is established, it's crucial to gather relevant information about the outage. This includes understanding the symptoms and impact of the issue, such as which services or applications are affected, the duration of the problem, and the number of users impacted. Information gathering might involve querying end-users, checking monitoring systems, and reviewing logs.

CLI commands can be invaluable at this stage for gathering real-time data about network devices and services. For example, using the **ping** command to test connectivity to key devices or using **traceroute** to identify the path packets take through the network can provide valuable insights into the issue's scope and location.

After gathering initial information, the next step is to categorize the outage based on its severity and impact.

Network outages are often classified into different severity levels, such as minor, major, or critical, depending on the extent of disruption and the importance of the affected services. Categorization helps prioritize efforts and allocate resources effectively.

It's essential to assemble a cross-functional team with expertise in various areas, such as network engineering, system administration, security, and application support. This interdisciplinary approach ensures a comprehensive assessment of the problem and a more holistic resolution strategy.

Root cause analysis is a critical aspect of resolving complex network outages. Engineers must identify the underlying issue that led to the outage, which often involves investigating multiple layers of the network stack, including physical, data link, network, transport, and application layers. This process requires a deep understanding of network protocols and troubleshooting techniques.

CLI commands like **show** and **debug** can be instrumental in diagnosing network issues. For example, on Cisco devices, the **show interfaces** command provides detailed information about the status and statistics of network interfaces, helping engineers identify interface errors or congestion issues. Similarly, the **show ip route** command displays the routing table, aiding in identifying routing problems.

In addition to CLI commands, network monitoring tools and packet capture tools like Wireshark can be used to capture and analyze network traffic in real-time. This is particularly useful when investigating complex issues related to network congestion, packet loss, or abnormal traffic patterns.

Once the root cause is identified, the next step is to develop an action plan for resolving the outage. This plan should outline specific steps, tasks, and responsibilities for each team member involved. In some cases, it may be necessary to roll back recent changes or apply temporary workarounds to restore services while a permanent fix is implemented.

For example, if a network device configuration change is determined to be the root cause, the action plan may involve reverting to a known good configuration using CLI commands like **configure replace** on Cisco devices. Similarly, if a software bug is identified, a temporary fix may involve applying a software patch or update.

Throughout the resolution process, effective communication with stakeholders, including end-users, management, and IT support teams, is crucial. Providing regular updates on the progress of the resolution effort helps manage expectations and demonstrates transparency.

Testing and validation are essential steps before declaring the outage as fully resolved. Network engineers should verify that the services and applications impacted by the outage are functioning correctly and that performance is back to expected levels. CLI commands and monitoring tools can be used to confirm that the issue is indeed resolved.

Finally, a post-mortem or incident review should be conducted to analyze the outage's causes and identify areas for improvement. This process helps prevent similar incidents in the future and contributes to the organization's overall resilience.

In summary, complex network outage resolution is a multifaceted process that requires a systematic and collaborative approach. It involves gathering information, categorizing the severity, root cause analysis, action planning, effective communication, testing, and post-mortem analysis. CLI commands and network troubleshooting tools play a pivotal role in diagnosing and resolving complex network issues, ensuring the restoration of services and minimizing the impact on organizations and their users.

Root cause analysis (RCA) is a critical process in incident management that focuses on identifying the underlying causes of problems or incidents within a network or system. It is a structured approach aimed at preventing recurrence of incidents and improving overall system reliability.

When an incident occurs, it's essential to initiate the RCA process promptly. The first step is to assemble a cross-functional team comprising individuals with relevant expertise. This might include network engineers, system administrators, application developers, and security experts. The goal is to have a diverse set of skills and knowledge to thoroughly investigate the incident.

The team should begin by gathering all available data related to the incident. This includes logs, system performance metrics, configuration files, and any other relevant information. In the case of a network incident, CLI commands can be instrumental in collecting data from routers, switches, and other network devices. For example, the **show interface** command can provide insights into the status of network interfaces, while the **show log** command can reveal any error or warning messages.

Once the data is collected, the team can start the analysis process. The objective is to determine the immediate cause of the incident, such as a hardware failure, software bug, misconfiguration, or security breach. CLI commands can assist in this phase by allowing engineers to examine device and system logs for error messages or anomalies.

After identifying the immediate cause, the team must dig deeper to uncover the root cause. This involves tracing the incident's origin and understanding the sequence of events that led to the problem. For instance, if the incident is related to a network outage, engineers may use **traceroute** or **ping** commands to trace the path of network packets and identify where the communication broke down.

Throughout the RCA process, it's crucial to maintain a focus on the "Five Whys" principle. This technique involves asking "why" repeatedly to peel back the layers of causality until the underlying root cause is revealed. For instance, if the initial cause is determined to be a server crash, asking "why did the server crash?" might lead to answers related to high CPU usage, which can then prompt further questions about the specific process causing the CPU spike.

Once the root cause is identified, the team can develop a set of corrective actions or recommendations to address it. These actions are designed to prevent similar incidents in the future. CLI commands and configuration changes may be part of the corrective actions. For instance, if a misconfiguration is identified as the root cause, the team may use CLI commands to modify the configuration settings and apply best practices.

Implementing these corrective actions requires careful planning and coordination. Each action should be documented, including the specific changes made, the devices or systems affected, and the individuals responsible for executing them. This documentation ensures accountability and helps prevent errors during the implementation phase.

After implementing the corrective actions, it's essential to monitor the system or network to ensure that the incident does not recur. This involves ongoing performance monitoring, log analysis, and the use of network monitoring tools. CLI commands and scripts can be used to automate some of these monitoring tasks.

In addition to RCA, a post-incident review (PIR) or post-mortem is a critical part of the incident management process. The purpose of a PIR is to evaluate the organization's response to the incident, identify areas for improvement, and document lessons learned.

The PIR should involve the same cross-functional team that conducted the RCA, as well as key stakeholders and management. It's an opportunity to assess how well the incident was handled, whether the response procedures were followed, and whether there were any shortcomings in communication or decision-making.

CLI commands can play a role in the PIR by providing data on response times, system behavior during the incident, and the effectiveness of implemented changes. For example, engineers can use command-line tools to extract historical performance data, compare it to the incident timeline, and assess whether corrective actions have resulted in improvements.

The output of the PIR should include a comprehensive report that summarizes the incident, the RCA findings, the corrective actions taken, and recommendations for future incident prevention. This report is a valuable resource for organizations to continually improve their incident management processes and enhance system reliability.

In summary, root cause analysis and post-incident reviews are integral components of effective incident management. CLI commands and network troubleshooting techniques play a crucial role in both processes, from collecting data and identifying root causes to implementing corrective actions and monitoring ongoing performance. By following these structured approaches, organizations can enhance their incident response capabilities and reduce the likelihood of future incidents.

## Conclusion

In the ever-evolving world of networking, the TCP/IP protocol suite stands as the foundation upon which modern communication networks are built. The four-book bundle, "TCP/IP Network+ Protocols and Campus LAN Switching Fundamentals," has provided a comprehensive journey through the intricacies of TCP/IP networking, from the essential basics to advanced optimization and troubleshooting techniques.

In "TCP/IP Essentials: A Beginner's Guide," Book 1 served as the starting point for novices venturing into the realm of networking. It laid the groundwork by demystifying the TCP/IP protocol suite, IP addressing, and fundamental network concepts. This beginner's guide equipped readers with the essential knowledge required to understand and work with networking protocols.

"Network+ Protocols: Intermediate Insights," Book 2, expanded upon this foundation by delving deeper into networking protocols, subnetting techniques, and routing concepts. It bridged the gap between basic understanding and intermediate expertise, empowering readers with valuable insights into network design and management.

Book 3, "Advanced TCP/IP and Campus LAN Switching," elevated the discourse by exploring advanced topics in TCP/IP networking. It covered routing protocols, VLAN design, and high availability strategies, providing readers with the tools and knowledge needed to design, optimize, and secure complex networks.

The final installment, "Expert TCP/IP Optimization and Troubleshooting," Book 4, catered to the seasoned professionals seeking to refine their skills. It offered in-depth insights into network optimization, performance tuning, and intricate troubleshooting methodologies. By addressing real-world scenarios and challenges, this book elevated readers to an expert level of TCP/IP proficiency.

Collectively, these four books formed a comprehensive resource bundle that catered to readers at all levels of expertise. Whether you were a beginner taking your first steps into the world of networking or an experienced professional seeking to enhance your skills, this bundle offered something for everyone.

As we conclude this journey through TCP/IP networking, we hope that you've found these books to be valuable companions in your quest for knowledge and mastery in the field. Networking is a dynamic and ever-expanding discipline, and the skills and insights gained from these books will serve as a solid foundation for your ongoing exploration and growth in this exciting field.

In closing, we encourage you to continue your networking journey with a curious and innovative spirit. As technology continues to evolve, so too will the world of networking. Embrace the challenges, stay updated with emerging trends, and never stop learning. The knowledge you've gained from this bundle will empower you to navigate the complexities of modern networking and contribute to the ever-advancing world of information technology.